DISAPPEARING NEW MEXICO

*Photographic Tours of Ghost Towns
with Stories about the State's Past
and Some of Its Characters*

Mac Read
and
Manfred Laendle

ISBN 9798370068119

Library of Congress Cataloging in Publication Data

Read, John M. and Laendle, Manfred
        Disappearing New Mexico

Photographs by Mac Read and Manfred Laendle

Includes bibliographical references and index

1. Ghost towns - NewMexico - Guidebooks
2. New Mexico History
3. Automobile Travel

For

Beth, David, Elizabeth, Kathy,

Monika, and Mulkie

Table of Contents

Southeastern Counties

Southwestern Counties

Southwestern Counties (continued)

Introduction

"Disappearing New Mexico" is a collection of short, illustrated articles about the many ghost towns in the state. It is intended to be a guidebook for tourists and locals alike. It is profusely illustrated with photographs. None of the photographs were obtained from historical archives. They are all modern. This book differs from previous guides in that it doesn't dwell on deceased people who will not be known to the reader. Instead, we focus on ghost towns that are accessable today to bring these ghost towns to life for the modern visitor.

There is a chapter on the civil war in the west. The importance of the war in the west is largely unknown to people in the east. However, the United States Congress declared the Battle of Glorieta one of the ten most significant battles of the war.

Many old ghost towns are hard to find being behind locked gates or completely destroyed. Here, we concentrate on ghost towns you can visit today. With only a few exceptions, these are reachable without the aid of a high clearance vehicle. Each section contains driving directions. You will not need a GPS. But for a single exception, all the photographs were made recently. Until these sites disappear, and it will happen to some, you can go there and expect to see the same structures.

The definition of a ghost town requires a bit of discussion. There are, indeed, ghost towns that are completely deserted. However, most still have a few residents. Some ghost towns even have a population of nearly a thousand persons. What is common to all is that the original reason for the town's existence is gone or has substantially declined. So have the people.

In many western towns mining was the reason for existence. In most cases, the town and its buildings were owned by the mining company. When the mine closed, the town was dismantled or sold. The people left to find other work. Madrid is an example of this. The entire town, equipment, and mineral rights were offered for sale. There were no takers, but the buildings were later bought by individuals. There are still other towns where the mine petered out and the buildings were just abandoned.

Transportation was responsible for the birth of many towns. Transportation also caused many of these same towns to die. For example, Yeso was a train stop when the steam locomotive was king. Engines stopped there to pick up water. With the coming of the diesel engine, water wasn't needed. Once Yeso contained a large number of abandoned stone buildings. However, in the short period of six years, many of these old stone structures have disappeared. Cuervo, which prospered when US-66 came through, is another very visible example.

Other factors that hastened the demise of these ghost towns included floods and government regulations. Guadalupe was done in by both floods and government regulations . War is another. World War II took young people away from their villages. After experiencing city life, many never returned to the farms and ranches. Lastly, government, in protecting one resource, often changed or destroyed another.

This book doubtlessly contains errors, for which we take full responsibility. However, there is conflicting or sketchy documentation on several subjects. It is frequently difficult to know which, if either, is correct. For example, did Billy the Kid really die at Fort Sumner?

Organization of This Book

There are many ways to divide New Mexico into manageable regions. Indeed, it seems each department in the state government has its own method. The one used here is probably the simplest. We divided the state into four quadrants, admittedly of unequal size. The northern ones are generally north of I-40, but Torrance and Guadalupe are also south of I-40. We chose to lump them in with the northeast. Likewise, we generally used the Rio Grande to divide east from west. However, we tried not to let the river split counties. This separation is arbitrary, but New Mexico is a huge state. It is unlikely that anyone could or would explore any two quadrants in a single day.

Each quadrant is organized by county, with counties north and west being presented first. Within each county the order of the sites is alphabetical.

Highway Designations

We have chosen to identify roads in New Mexico with letters, followed by a hyphen, and a number. The letters designate the responsible authority. Thus, I-25 is Interstate 25; US-84 is US 84; state roads are SR, with SR-14, being theTurquoise Trail that goes south from Santa Fe and past Cerrillos; and CR-119 is County Road 119. It links Anton Chico to US-84.

Northwestern Counties

Gramerco (McKinley County)

The abandoned mine is north of Gallup off US-491.

In 1920 the Gallup American Coal Company started sinking mine shafts in the area. When the mines closed in the 1960s, the railroad spur was removed. The power plant was decommissioned a bit later. With a population of about 2,000, one can't really call Gramerco a ghost town, but it has certainly seen more prosperous days.

Abiquiú (Rio Arriba County)

Abiquiú is about 48 miles north of Santa Fe. Take US-84/285 north to Espanola. Just as you get into Espanola, the two highways make a left turn and cross the Rio Grande (going straight takes you to Taos). Turn right at the light after you cross the river. Go about one block and then merge left. You are still on US-84/285. You may have trouble finding it, but Hernandez contains Ansel Adam's famous "Moonrise" church.

US-285 splits off the right at La Chuachia. Go straight on US-84. A few miles after the intersection with Hwy-55 (to El Rito) you will see the ruins of Santa Rosa de Lima on the right, where there you will see a small parking area.

The village of Abiquiú lies ahead. This is where one meets for a tour of Georgia O'Keeffe's house. Tour reservations are made through the O'Keeffe Museum in Santa Fe.

The Abiquiu Inn serves very fine meals, and Bode's General Store offers sandwiches, cold drinks, and restrooms. To get to Abiquiú village, turn left opposite Bode's and

Disappearing New Mexico

drive up the hill on Hwy-187, past the post office.

Further north on US-84 one can find Abiquiu Lake, Ghost Ranch, Christ in the Desert Monastery, and Echo Amphitheater.

Abiquiú isn't exactly a ghost town[50]. It has a population of about 230 people. It has a post office, a very busy general store (Bode's), an art gallery, a hotel/restaurant, seveval art studios and Saint Thomas the Apostle Catholic Church. Many families live in the area, and call Abiquiú home. Abiquiú has thousands of visitors each year. Georgia O'Keeffe's house is a major attraction. It's across the street from the church and behind a stucco wall. The ruins of several adobe structures can also be seen.

Saint Thomas the Apostle Church

Palvadera Road, the drive past O'Keeffe's house, turns to the right and goes uphill. The Morada, with its several crosses, is at the curve as it goes uphill.

Plaza Blanca, Georgia O'Keeffe's White Place, is across the river, on the opposite side of the US-82. It is a major attraction. Be warned: Plaza Blanca now has a locked gate. There is a phone at the gate where you may call to gain admission.

A good way to get to Plaza Blanca is to drive back to SR-554 and then take a second left onto CR-155.

Santa Rosa de Lima (Rio Arriba County)

Santa Rosa de Lima was settled by the Spanish in the early part of the 18th century. By 1744, about 20 families were living in the area, where they founded a community known as Plaza de Santa Rosa de Lima. The community, which was constantly harassed by Comanche raids, was finally abandoned in 1747. Today, even the ruins of the village are gone.

The adobe church was built around 1744 and was in use until the 1930s. The roof has collapsed and it is now in ruins. There are also several crosses on the ground behind the church. The old church is interesting. It seems to invite passersby on the highway to stop and visit. If you do stop, please be careful of the building's walls. They are very fragile.

The church property is private. It belongs to the Archdiocese of Santa Fe. In 1978, Santa Rosa de Lima was added to the National Register of Historic Places.

The Ruins of Santa Rosa de Lima

Plaza Blanca can be seen in the background, behind the old church.

Disappearing New Mexico

El Rito (Rio Arriba County)

Turn on to NM-554 from US-84 It's 3.3 miles south of Abiquiú.

El Rito shouldn't be classified as a ghost town. Families live in and around it. It has also become a bit of an artist community. It houses buildings for the Northern New Mexico Community College, as well as the offices of the El Rito Ranger District of the Carson National Forest Service.

The Community College seems to be in one of those sad cases where they have a beautiful facility, but too few students to keep it open.

Locals claim the Church of San Nepomucenio is the oldest church in New Mexico (left). It is still in use and very much alive. It was restored in 1980. *Noie: the San Miguel Chapel in Santa Fe is generally recognized as the oldest church in the continental US (1610 AD).*

Church of San Nepomucenio

Many of El Rito's shops are in sad shape.

Barn at East End of Town

A Storefront for Sale

If you are visiting at lunch time, try El Farolito (corner of the right most image above). It enjoys a good reputation.

San Luis (Sandoval County)

The next few areas are best reached from Bernalillo. From I-25 take US-550 north to CR-279. Turn left and travel about 7 miles. The church is on the left. A morada is across the road and up against the cliff.

San Luis Church

San Luis is a small community of about sixty people. The San Luis Catholic Church is on the left side of the road, with it's rear facing the road. The cemetery is to the front of the church. Up by the cliff, on the north side of CR-279, is another morada.

Morada on North Side of CR-279

Disappearing New Mexico

Cabezon Peak (Sandoval County)

Cabezon peak is a very imposing volcanic plug that can be seen from US-550. It lies southwest of San Luis. Cabezon plays a part in the Navajo creation story. It is said that the Hero Twins[40], *Nayenezgani* and *To'badzistsini*, killed *Ye'iitsoh*, the monster who was eating the people. They cut off his head and threw it over *Tsooddzil* (Mount Taylor). The Peak is the monster's head, wth head down and neck up. The monster's blood is said to have run downhill and congealed to form the dark lava fields around Grants.

Cabezon rises to 7,785 feet, nearly 2,000 feet above the valley floor. The plug was formed when magma of the old volcano solidified, and the surrounding sediment eroded away. Cabezon means "big head" in Spanish. Cabezon is a popular climbing spot.

Guadalupe (Sandoval County)

Continue on 279 and you will find a turn to the south. This road goes to the base of Cabezon. Instead, continue west for about 2.5 miles. There will be another fork. This time, take the turn to the left. In about a mile, the elevation drops to provide a spectacular view of the canyon.

About a mile past is a view of the canyon. Further on, a concrete bridge crosses the Rio Puerco. Sometimes there is water in the river. At other times there is little or none. Incidentally, the name Rio Puerco can be a bit confusing since Puerco means pig in Spanish. Less common meanings include muddy, filthy, dirty, etc. The Rio Puerco continues south and joins the Rio Grande south of Belen.

From the bridge, continue south until you reach the Cabezon ghost town. Along the way you will see two rather distinctive peaks on your left. Cerro de Santa Clara is the northernmost and Cerro de Guadalupe the southern. They both appeared on New Mexico's 2012 centennial stamp. It's unlikely that even one percent of the state's population has seen these two peaks.

Cerro de Santa Clara

Cerro de Guadalupe

Disappearing New Mexico

Guadalupe Ghost Town (Sandoval County)

On the left, as you drive into Guadalupe[41,42], you will see the ruins of Juan Cordova's building, with the store on the first floor and living space on the second. Looking back, one sees Cabezon in the distance. On the right side of the road there are a number of adobe structures. These once housed about 200 people and their belongings. We were particularly amused by the building that used a Coca-Cola sign as a partial roof. Behind these buildings there is a recent metal structure.

Once, the Rio Puerco valley was a successful area for raising cattle. Unfortunately, drought struck in the early 1930's, killing about half the cattle. In 1934, Congress passed the Taylor Grazing Act, which regulated grazing on public lands. To satisfy the law, large numbers of cattle had to be destroyed. In 1938, a final blow to Guadalupe came when the log dam north of the village broke. This cost Guadalupe its source of water. The Federal Government refused to help rebuild the dam. The lack of water, the draw of city employment, and the hardships of life in the valley sealed Guadalupe's fate. By 1958, the school, the post office and the store had all closed.

Juan Cordova's Store and Residence - with Cabezon in the Distance

Many of the buildings were adobe, but some people added a bit of color, like the Coca-Cola roof.

Guadalupe Great House (Sandoval County)

This extension of the trip is NOT RECOMMENDED if the road is the least bit wet. Even then, a high-clearance vehicle with four-wheel drive is suggested. The road past the Guadalupe ghost town dips a considerable distance, and it can be completely washed away by heavy rains. Since cell phone coverage here is marginal, rescue could be a long time coming.

If you are determined, continue driving for about a mile past the dip. The Great House is at the top of a mesa on your left (image on page 10). A small parking area is by the road. To reach the Great House you will need to hike the trail to the top of the mesa and then turn right.

Disappearing New Mexico

A large number of turquoise flakes have been found around the Wijij Great House in Chaco Canyon, suggesting the area was used to produce turquoise jewelry. Furthermore, spectrographic analysis of the flakes has identified Cerrillos (next page) as the source of the turquoise.

The Guadalupe Great House is about half-way between Cerrillos and Chaco. Since the mineral would have been hand carried over 170 miles on foot, a half-way house makes sense. Of course, like everything about Chaco, this idea is subject to debate.

The Guadalupe Great House is the easternmost Anasazi great house. To reach the great house follow the trail on the south side of the mesa. When you reach the top turn right. The path climbs slightly and leads to the relatively flat eastern edge of the mesa. The roof covering the great kiva is typical of Anasazi excavations.

Roof Protectng the Great Kiva

Mesa with Great House on Top

View Inside the Great Kiva

Cabezon Through a Window

The Remains of a Circular Kiva

Cerrillos (Santa Fe County)

Going south from Santa Fe on SR-14 (the Turquoise Trail), Cerrillos is 14.7 miles south of I-25. Turn right at the first road past the railroad tracks (Main Street). Be sure to check out the Turquoise Mining Museum at the northwest end of Waldo Street.

Going north from I-40, go to the intersection with NM-14 and turn north. In getting to Cerrellos you will pass through several other semi-ghost towns including Golden and Madrid. Cerrellos is 31.5 miles north of I-40.

Today, it's hard to imagine that this sleepy little town[43] of 230 people once had a population of 2,500. In 1879, gold was discovered around Cerrillos and turquoise was re-discovered. The town exploded with prospectors and investors. At one point, the town had over twenty five saloons, four hotels, a school, and two churches. By the turn of the century, with its mineral wealth exhausted, mines started closing. In 1890 fire destroyed many of the original buildings. Much of Cerrillos has the look of an old cowboy town. In fact, several western movies, including *"Young Guns"*,

Disappearing New Mexico

were filmed here. Cerrillos is a gem. Don't miss it.

Of historical interest, former Governor Lew Wallace stayed at a hotel in Cerrillos (since burned) while he read and corrected galley proofs for his famous novel, *"Ben-Hur"*.

The Clear Light Opera House (left) existed as early as 1881. In 1903 the building was sold to the Cerrillos Masonic Lodge for $305.

The Casa Grande Trading Post (right) has an interesting collection of minerals, old tools, machinery and houeshold goods.

They also have an assortment of barnyard birds and they sell feed. The kids might enjoy feeding them.

Mary's Bar is a Long-standing Cerrillos Fixture

St Joseph Catholic Church

For an interesting look at a faded past, turn left on either Anthracite or Cerrillos Heights Roads (opposite side of Hwy 14 from Cerrillos). Drive up behind the houses. You will find the remains of an elegant old high school, complete with amphitheater, stone sculpture, and a gymnasium.

Ceramic Sculpture Out Front

Old High School with Amphitheater

Waldo (Santa Fe County)

From I-25 take exit 267 to CR-57 and follow it toward Cerrillos. About 6-7 miles from I-25 you will find a parking lot, along with some low concrete structures and gate leading to the railroad tracks. The coke ovens are to the right on the other side of the tracks.

Coming from Cerrillos, take First Street, cross the railroad tracks and turn left onto CR-57 (it's dirt). Parking is about 2-2.5 miles away. The view at Waldo canyon is worth a picture.

Waldo never was much of a real town. Tracks for the Santa Fe Railroad ran through it, and a spur line was run from Waldo to Madrid so coal could be shipped to market. Since coal was plentiful and transportation was present, coke ovens were built at Waldo.

Coke Ovens

Disappearing New Mexico

Madrid (Santa Fe County)

Going south from Santa Fe on NM-14 (the Turquoise Trail), Madrid is 18.4 miles south of I-25, and 3 miles south of Cerrillos.

Going north from I-40, go east to the intersection with NM-14, and then turn north. On the way to Madrid NM-14 passes through the ghost town of Golden. Madrid is 28.5 miles north of I-40.

Madrid[44] has had two lives. One as the mining town that produced both anthracite and bituminous coal, and the other as the artsy community of today. It has a main drag filled with galleries and boutiques. Between the two times, NM-14 was lined with the remnants of coal company houses. Today, it's hard to find one of these houses. Madrid appeals to people who don't care for city living. It has a population of about 205 people.

Madrid was a major coal mining town in the early 20th century, but coal demand declined in the late 1940's. Its last shipment went to Los Alamos just before the lab switched to natural gas. The coal mine's owner, Oscar Huber, placed an ad in the Wall Street Journal. He offered the town, the buildings, the mines, the equipment, and the mineral rights for $250,000. There were no buyers. Properties were later purchased by individuals.

The Mine Shaft Tavern is a popular place to eat and drink. Entertainment is frequently avalable.

The movie, "Wild Hogs", staring John Tranvolta, turned Madrid into a must see place for bikers.

The scale in front of this modern business might surprise many visitors. It was used to weigh coal cars before they were shipped.

Many of the people in Madrid continue to have their mail delivered to boxes along Hwy-14 in town.

The Madrid Cemetery

Going south from Santa Fe on NM-14 and shortly after entering town, turn left onto Cave Road. Cave turns right at the end of the block. Continue on Cave Road, and turn right at the intersection with Black Road, which will intersect Waldo Mesa Road. Turn right onto Waldo Mesa. Keep to the right at the fork at Miller Gulch Road. The cemetery is on your right. The old section is first, with the newer one left.

The older section of the cemetery contains wooden grave markers that were typical in the west. Grave markers in the newer section tends to reflect the interests and/or personalities of the people buried there.

Disappearing New Mexico

Golden (Santa Fe County)

Golden is 30 miles south of I-25 at Santa Fe along NM-14, and 11 miles south of Madrid.

Going north from I-40, take Exit 175; follow Route 66 east to the intersection with NM-14, and then turn north. Golden is about 17 miles north of I-40.

When placer gold was discovered on Tuerto Creek in 1825, Golden hosted the first gold rush west of the Mississippi. However, at that time both the Mexican government and the Catholic Church claimed a large percentage of the findings. People may have kept their discoveries to themselves.

Formed in 1879, Golden was the center of the gold mining district. It supported saloons, businesses, a school, and even a stock exchange. Small-scale mining continued until about 1892. By 1928, mining had all but disappeared. The population declined, and the post office closed. Even though a few residents remained, Golden was officially a ghost town.

Remains of the Old Schoolhouse at Golden

Abandoned Houses in Golden

The San Francisco Catholic Church, the old schoolhouse, and several ruined dwellings are still of interest. Henderson Store is worth a stop. It's a modern facility that sells snacks and cold drinks, as well as jewelry, pottery, and Indian rugs.

Gate to San Francisco de Asis Catholic Church

..........Henderson Store in Golden (above)

Inside the Church (left)

Hagen (Sandoval County)

Take I-25 to San Filipe's Black Mesa Casino (Exit 252) and drive past the Casino and the track. Hagen is on the left, about 8 miles up the dirt road.

You may also reach Hagen from CR-14 by turning onto Puertocito Road about three miles south of Golden. In another three miles make a right turn at the crossroads and drive ten miles. Watch for the remains of Hagen on the right

Hagen first failed as a coal-mining town in 1908[45]. But in 1919 Dr. Justin De-Praslin convinced investors to contribute nearly $750,000 to revitalize the mine.

Disappearing New Mexico

Modern brick and concrete structures were built, and a rail spur was completed. The venture was soon shipping coal. The mines shut down in 1939 after hitting a huge layer of shale. Shortly thereafter, the rail spur closed.

Hagen is on private property, and it is POSTED. You can view the remains of the power plant, general store, and other buildings from the road.

View of Hagen from the Road

Elizabethtown (Colfax County)

Elizabethtown is on the "Enchanted Circle". It can be found by driving about five miles north of Eagle Nest on NM-38. Eagle Nest is on US-64 east of Taos (31 miles) or west of Raton (69 miles).

Elizabethtown can also be reached by driving the "Enchanted Circle" in reverse by going north from Taos and turning east on NM-38 at Questa. This takes you through Red River, with its in town ski slope and by the Enchanted Forest Cross Country Ski area.

While in the area, you may find a drive down Cimarron Canyon (US-64) worthwhile. In places, the canyon walls look like gigantic Roman columns stacked side-by-side.

The museum at Elizabethtown is open in the summer, other times you should call to check on hours.

Elizabethtown[46], often called E-town, began in 1866 with the discovery of gold on Willow Creek. It reached a peak population of 7,000 in 1870. In 1868, John Moore and a few others established a town on property once owned by Lucian Maxwell. Moore named the town after his daughter, Elizabeth.

Due to the scarcity of water, an army engineer was employed to study the possibility of diverting water from the Red River. The Moreno Water and Mining Company was formed to build the "Big Ditch", which was constructed between May and November of 1868. It covered forty miles and there were as many as 420 men working at one time. The cost was $300,000 ($6.3 million in 2022 dollars). In 1868, Elizabethtown had about a hundred buildings, including five stores, seven saloons, two hotels, three dance halls, and a drug store.

Along with prosperity came a significant amount of notoriety. There were shootings, lynchings, beatings, and murders. Violence was not unusual in western mining towns, but 'E-town' went over the top. Joseph Herberger and his gang of vigilantes, "Pony" O'Neal, Ned O'Hara, "Wall" Henderson, and Charles Kennedy were some of the notorious ones.

Elizabethtown had several firsts. It was the first incorporated town in New Mexico. For a brief while it was also the seat of Colfax County. However, by 1872 prosperity was declining, and the town's population shrank to about 100.

The town revived in the 1890s because the new railroad made mining feasible again. In 1903 a fire burned most of the town, and by 1917 mining had essentially ceased. 'E-town' was dead.

Magnificent arched windows appear in many photographs showing the remains of Elizabethtown's Mutz Hotel (it's been called other names also). Don't

Disappearing New Mexico

expect this scene today. Those pictured walls collapsed long ago. However, portions of the walls are still present, along with a huge pile of brick rubble, and an enormous chimney. The old hotel overlooks the beautiful valley below.

Mutz Hotel

Old Truck Announcing Elizabethtown

It has been said that if you have to be buried, the Elizabethtown Cemetery is the only proper place. This beautiful and peaceful spot overlooks the Moreno Valley and the west side of Baldy Mountain. It's hard to beat.

Northeastern Counties

Cimarron (Colfax County)

Cimarron is on US-64, 24 miles west of Eagle Nest. The road passes through Cimarron Canyon, with spectacular cliff faces that resemble bundles of Roman columns.

Cimarron can also be reached by driving 42 miles west from Raton on US-64.

A third way to Cimarron is to take exit 419 from I-25 and turn west onto NM-58. Cimarron is about 19 miles from the interstate.

The Santa Fe Trail was America's first international trade highway. From 1821, and for nearly sixty years, until replaced by railroads, it played a significant role in America's westward expansion. The trail started in or near Independence, Missouri and terminated in Santa Fe. The trail was relatively uneventful in the first part, but west of Dodge City, Kansas it split into two trails, offering teamsters a choice.

The Jornada Route (Cimarron Cutoff) was over dry desert. It crossed the Cimarron and Arkansas rivers before reaching La Junta (now Watrus) in New Mexico. Along the way it passed through the western tip of Oklahoma and by the modern towns of Clayton, Springer, and Wagon Mound. This route saved about ten days, relative to the alternative.

The Mountain Route was longer, but it had water - very important if one was moving livestock. This route followed the Arkansas River to Fort Lyon, Colorado and turned south through Trinidad, Colorado, only to make the difficult mountain crossing at Raton Pass. From there it turned west toward Cimarron, and then proceeded on south to La Junta. In addition to lack of water, attacks from Indians along the Cimarron Cutoff made the mountain route popular with traders, immigrants, gold-seekers, and government supply trains.

In 1842 Lucian B. Maxwell[26,47] came to the Beaubien-Miranda Ranch in northern New Mexico, courted and married Luz Beaubien, one of the owner's daughters. Maxwell eventually inherited the 1,714,765-acre ranch, part of a Mexican Land grant.

Maxwell's Aztec Mill

Disappearing New Mexico

The Lambert Inn, later renamed the St. James Hotel, was built in 1872 by Henri Lambert, who had been a personal chef to Abraham Lincoln. Trying to find gold, Lambert had first settled in Elizabethtown, but had no luck in that venture. Maxwell, who also owned Elizabethtown, encouraged Lambert to move to Cimarron and open the lodge.

The Lambert Inn played host to lawmen and outlaws alike, including: the Earp brothers, Buffalo Bill Cody, Lew Wallace (Governor and author of Ben Hur), Annie Oakley, Zane Grey, Jesse James, and Black Jack Ketchum. Many people were killed in the Lambert. The hotel is said to be haunted by the ghosts of those killed.

In 1852, Maxwell built a very large mansion on the site of the town. The town was

Front of the St. James Hotel

chartered as Cimarron in 1859. In Spanish, the name signifies wild or unbroken, i.e., a mustang. In 1864 Maxwell also built the Aztec Mill which is preserved as a museum. The well-known Philmont Scout Ranch is south of Cimarron on NM-21.

Rayado (Colfax County)

Rayado is 11 miles south of Cimarron on NM-21. The road passes through the Philmont Scout Ranch.

From I-25 you can reach Rayado by taking exit 412 or 414, going into Springer and turning west onto NM-21. This road takes you through some beautiful grasslands, as well

Rayado, founded by Lucien Maxwell[48] in 1848, was the first permanent settlement in Colfax County. Lucian Maxwell was also the third largest landowner in U.S. history (1.7 million acres). In 1844 Maxwell came to Taos, New Mexico, where he married Carlos Beaubien's daughter, Luz Beaubien. In 1843, Carlos Beaubeim and his partner had received a sizable land grant. Kit Carson married Josefa Jaramillo, also of Mexican decent, at about the same time.

In 1849, at the conclusion of the Mexican-American War, Maxwell and Carson proposed building a fort on the Rayado River at Rayado, New Mexico. The site is along the Santa Fe Trail. In the early days, Indian raids were common around Rayado, and it was difficult to attract other settlers to the area. Maxwell built a large house and Carson built a smaller adobe hut. Carson continued to maintain his house in Taos, where Josefa spent most of her time.

Maxwell's house is on the southern corner of what is now the Philmont Scout Ranch. It is along the Cimarron Cutoff of the Santa Fe Trail coming from Fort Leavenworth, Kansas. Maxwell's house is on the west side of the road. As seen in the photograph, Maxwell's house is still in excellent repair. Across the street is a small Catholic Church.

Maxwell's House in Rayado

The Kit Carson Museum is located 300-400 feet south of Lucian Maxwell's house. The museum is a recreation of Carson's house, and it has maintained some of the original adobe walls. Exhibits include a stagecoach and covered wagon, along with many examples of necessities for living in 1850's. Both are

Wilt Child Church at Rayado

Disappearing New Mexico

owned and operated by the Philmont Scout Ranch. There are guided tours to Carson's Museum, which is open from June 10 to August 25. Call 575-376-2281 for more information.

Kit Cartson's Compound at Rayado

In 1850, the Army moved its fort 30 miles (48 km) further south to Fort Union. Maxwell sold his Rayado property and moved to Cimarron, where he built the Aztec Mill.

Dawson (Colfax County)

Drive 12.5 miles east of Cimarron on US 64, turning north at the sign for the cemetery. Drive another 4.5 miles on the dirt road (A-38).

From I-25, take exit 446 onto US-64. Drive 22.2 miles toward Cimarron. Turn right onto A-38.

In 1869 John Dawson purchased 1,000 acres of land on the Vermejo River from Lucian Maxwell[49]. The price was $3,700. Dawson's intention was to raise cattle. Soon after settling there, he found chunks of coal on the surface of his land. He decided to burn the coal rather than wood. Seeing this, neighbors asked if they could try some. They liked it and Dawson started supplementing his ranching business by selling coal. The coal business was born.

In 1870 Lucian Maxwell sold his interest in the Maxwell Land Grant to an English firm. It quickly changed hands several times. In 1872 a Dutch company, planning to exploit the mineral resources purchased the land. Part of their plan was to evict squatters that Maxwell had allowed to live on his property. They also tried to evict Dawson. but, he hired an attorney and took the matter to court. Dawson won, and in the process, the court found that Dawson had unknowingly purchased 20,000 acres.

In 1901 Dawson sold the property to the Dawson Fuel Company for $400,000. By August, fifty miners were ready to work. A sawmill was producing lumber for houses and other buildings. Also a 137-mile rail line was being run to Tucumcari. In Tucumcari it linked into the Rock Island Line and provided Dawson with a greatly expanded market. Dawson was quickly becoming the largest coal-mining site in New Mexico, and it was on its way to being one of the largest mines in the U.S.

On September 14, 1903, a fire broke out in Stags Canyon Mine #1. The fire was followed by several explosions. Five hundred miners escaped. Three were killed.

By 1905 the town had a population of 2,000, along with a post office, a liquor store, a mercantile, a hotel, a school, and a newspaper.

In 1906 the Phelps Dodge Corporation bought the mines and was determined to make Dawson a model mining town. They built the four-story brick Phelps Dodge Mercantile, which sold food, clothing, shoes, hardware, furniture, drugs, jewelry, baked goods, and ice. The hospital was staffed with five doctors. It had a laboratory, a surgery, and x-ray facilities.

The company provided a movie theater, swimming pool, bowling alley, baseball park, pool hall, golf course, lodge hall, and an opera house. There were both Catholic and Protestant churches, as well as two elementary schools and a large high school. The schools employed forty teachers and served 1,200 students. The company also built a steam-powered generator that provided electricity, not only to Dawson, but also to Raton and other nearby communities, including Walsenburg, Colorado.

Disappearing New Mexico

In its heyday, Dawson had ten operating mines. It produced enough coal to heat one-sixth of the United States. With a population of 9,000, it was one of the largest towns in New Mexico, perhaps exceeded only by Albuquerque and Santa Fe. Dawson's amenities attracted miners from all over the world. Its ethnic mix included Greeks, Italians, Austrians, Chinese, Polish, Irish, French, Germans, Britons, Finns, Slavs, Swedes, and Mexicans. Houses rented for as little as $8.50 per month.

Dawson was impressive in other surprising ways. It had:
- three schools
- 40 schoolteachers
- a movie theater
- a swimming pool
- a golf course
- a world-class department store
- a baseball team
- and some of the largest coal mines in the US

On October 21, 1913, state mine inspectors examined the Stag Canyon Mine #2, and declared it safe. The next day an explosion in that mine killed 263 workers, making it the second worst mine disaster in U.S. history. The problem wasn't with the inspection. Someone set off explosives while workers were still in the mine. The mines ventilation system was not adequate to clear the gases.

Cemetary at Dawson

On February 8, 1923, a second explosion, this time in Stag Canyon Mine #1, killed another 123 men.

A Few Larger Graves Markers

Another View of Grave Makers

The mines continued to operate for anther thirty years, but the demand for coal declined. In 1950, Phelps Dodge closed the Dawson mines and sold the entire property to the National Iron and Metals Company, who were contracted to dismantle it. Some of the houses and buildings have been moved, and the entire town has been razed. Today, all a visitor sees is the cemetery where miners and others are buried. White iron crosses mark the miner's graves. The land has since been sold. Now it is part of a working ranch.

On April 9, 1992, the cemetery at Dawson was added to the National Register of Historic Places, being one of the few cemeteries to be included. The tragic explosions contributed to its inclusion, but the huge ethnic mix of those interred there was a major factor.

Disappearing New Mexico

Johnson Mesa (Colfax County)

To reach Johnson Mesa from Raton, take Hwy-71, where St. Johns Church is at the intersection with A-48, about 17 miles from Raton.

Alternatively, St. Johns Church is about 19 miles from Folsom, along Hwy-17.

The road to the Yankee mining area is about three miles west of St. Johns. Those mines closed in the 1920s. The land is now a private ranch and is closed to the public.

The land around St. Johns Methodist Episcopal Church is both very beautiful and incredibly lonely. Johnson Mesa rises about 1,800 feet above the valley floor at Raton. The mesa top, which is about fourteen miles long, is covered by grasslands and gentle hills. The mesa is named for Lige Johnson who settled and let his cattle graze there in the late 1800's.

In the late 1880's Marion Bell led a group of fellow railroad workers there to try their hand at farming. The people raised potatoes, oats, and other crops. Later, some turned to cattle ranching. The community known as Bell grew and even added a post office. There were five schools, including a high school. Yankee, an abandoned mining area, now a private ranch, is a few miles away.

St. Johns Methodist Episcopal Church

The St Johns Methodist Episcopal Church was constructed 1897-1898. The church is now a Registered New Mexico Cultural Property. The church was used by all denominations in the area. The Johnson Mesa Cemetery is on the corner, opposite the church.

After World War I, people started leaving Johnson Mesa. At 8,000 - 8,400 feet elevation winters were harsh, and people were looking for an easier way to make a living. There are still a few families living on the mesa. Scattered ranches and cattle can be seen from the church.

As mentioned, the land is both very beautiful and very lonely. It agrees with some people, but not most. It's a long drive to the nearest grocery.

Yes, bullet holes still punctuate road signs here.

Disappearing New Mexico

Sugarite (Colfax County)

Take NM-72 east from Raton (exit 452 on I-25) and proceed about 10 miles. Turn left onto NM-526 and continue into Sugarite State Park. The ruins of the Ensign Mansion can be seen uphill on the right about a mile after turning onto NM-526.

In the hills and valleys, on either side of Raton, an immense quantity of coal was found. As a result, in the early part of the twentieth century many coal mines sprung up around Raton. These towns had names like Brilliant, Catskill, Gardner, Otero, Sugarite[51], Swastika (changed to Blossberg after Hitler came to power), and Yankee. They would still be great ghost towns to visit, but only Sugarite is open to the public. The other properties have been sold to private individuals and have become ranches or nature preserves. Sugarite is now a New Mexico State Park.

The coal camp, located in Chicoria Canyon, was settled in 1909. It was initially owned by the Chicoria Coal Company, but later came under control of the Rocky Mountain and Pacific Coal Company. At first, the coal was hauled by wagon to Raton where it was mostly used for home heating. In 1912 the company expanded operations. A one-room schoolhouse was opened that later was replaced by a two-room schoolhouse. The new school had a second-floor auditorium that was used for dances and motion pictures. By 1915 the town had grown to 500 residents.

As Sugarite grew, concrete and stone buildings were constructed along both sides of the canyon wall. The foundations of these are easily seen today. Soccer, football, and baseball were played. A clubhouse provided cultural programs, a soft drink bar, and a pool hall. A store also provided the many essentials, and there was a doctor on-site. The foundation of his house can still be seen.

In 1941, the Company announced the mines were closing. The 450 residents of Sugarite were given time to move. Many families chose to move to Raton. Their houses were moved for them.

When at Sugarite, stop by the Park Services Visitors' Center to get updated information. On the east side of canyon and behind the Visitors' Center, trails lead uphill. The "Town Loop Trail" contains many foundations, as well as a hornito style stone oven. Further up the hill are remains of mine buildings and equipment. The remains of the store, club house, and school are visible down by the river. This loop trail is easily walked.

The "Mine Trail" may be a struggle for some, but worthwhile for those who take it. There you will find the old dynamite shack, along with the #2 Mine which is closed. Further along the trail are the cable wheels that raised and lowered coal cars. The view from here, nearly 1,000 feet above the canyon floor, is rather spectacular.

Foundation of the Old School House

Mechanism for Raising and Lowering Coal Cars

Disappearing New Mexico

Abandoned Mine Building

Hornito Oven at Sugarite

Sugarite Canyon State Park was established in 1985. It receives about 125,000 visitors a year.

On arriving to or leaving Sugarite, about 1.2 miles from Route 72, look up hill toward the east. You may be able to see the ruins of a large mansion with a collapsing roof.

"Carisbrooke II" was a 20-room, 5-bathroom mansion built by A.D. Ensign on his 2,100-acre ranch in the late 1800's. With imported furniture, oriental rugs, replicas of famous artwork, including paintings and marble statues, the mansion was designed to attract wealthy vacationers from back east. Activities included hunting (bear, deer, pronghorn, and ducks), hiking, horseback riding, tennis, snowshoeing, and skiing. A stay there, including gourmet meals, was a bargain at $150 a month.

Activities at "Carisbrooke II" came to an "unexpected" end at a party one night in 1906. Both Mr. and Mrs. Ensign were taken away by unidentified men and were never seen again. It seems Mr. Ensign's money was acquired by persuading wealthy English women to invest in his ranch and then using the money himself. Was the abduction a payback, or carefully planned exit? Who knows?

Since closing, the ranch has been sold several times. One owner used the polished wooden floors for as a roller rink for local kids.

The Ruins of Carisbrooke II

Folsom (Union County)

From Raton, take Exit 451 from I-25 and turn east onto US-64/87. Continue for 27 miles to the town of Capulin. Turn north onto NM-325 and drive nine miles to Folsom. The drive takes you past the Capulin Mountain National Monument. In Folsom the museum is at the intersection of Grand Avenue (NM-325) and Gratz Street. Return to Raton by taking Gratz to NM-72 and turning on to it. This road takes you across the beautiful, but lonely, Johnson Mesa.

Folsom is a small village (about 56 people) in Union County, a few miles north of the Capulin Volcano National Monument. The area is known for the flash flood of 1908. The flood ravaged the town, but it also swept soil from the banks of an arroyo eight miles west and uncovered a monumental archaeological find.

On August 27, 1908, a massive thunderstorm dumped thirteen inches of rain on Johnson Mesa above the town. It produced flooding that killed 18 people and nearly destroyed the town. Someone at the Crowfoot Ranch saw or heard the wall of water coming down the Dry Cimarron River. They knew the town was in danger and alerted the telephone operator in Folsom.

The operator, Sarah J. "Sally" Rooke, stayed at her station and called the residents to warn them. She was swept eight miles downstream. Telephone operators from across the country contributed 4,334 dimes to honor their colleague. The memorial stands at the corner of Main Street and Folsom Avenue.

Disappearing New Mexico

Folsom Museum – Occasionally Open in Summer

After the flood, George McJunkin[17], a self-educated ex-slave, cowboy, and ranch foreman discovered an assembly of large bones sticking out from the banks of Dead Horse Arroyo. McJunkin, who had a keen interest in science, took the bones home and studied them. They resembled buffalo bones, but he decided they were too large to be from a modern buffalo. In the same layer of dirt, he also found flint artifacts, including chips and points. He concluded that prehistoric buffalo had been killed and butchered at the site thousands of years ago.

McJunkin's conclusions differed from scientific opinion of the time. Dr. Aleš Hrdlička, curator of physical anthropology at the Smithsonian, was the leading authority on the age of living things in North America. Hrdlička firmly believed that Homo sapiens had only been on the planet for about 6,000 years. Hrdlička's position at the Smithsonian, and as editor of the Journal of Physical Anthropology at the Smithsonian, was the leading authority on the age of living things in North America. Hrdlička's position made him a difficult man to argue with. Those that did were often ridiculed brutally. As a result, very few paid attention to McJunkin's discovery.

In 1908, the Crowfoot Ranch was sold, but McJunkin stayed on as foreman. He

Dead Horse Arroyo - Photo by Nancy Melin

and the new owner's son, Ivan Shoemaker, dug more bones. This time, they also found a fluted lance point in the same stratum of the bank. These were sent to the Colorado Museum of Natural History (now the Denver Museum). The next spring Jesse Figgins, the museum's director, sent paleontologist Harold Cook to Crowfoot.

McJunkin helped him with exploratory digging. However, not much else happened at Crowfoot for a long time.

In 1921, McJunkin became ill with dropsy or edema - a buildup of fluid in the body's tissues. This can be very painful. When McJunkin could no longer "cowboy", he moved to the lean-to room at the back of the Folsom Hotel. He drank whiskey to ease the pain. Ivan would come to the hotel and read to him. In 1922, McJunkin died, never learning of the outcome or the significance of his discovery. He was buried in the cemetery there.

In 1926, Figgins became personally involved in the Folsom site. During the summer of 1927, four lance points were discovered, but these were loose in the clay that contained bones. When a fifth point was found Figgins stopped the dig and called several prominent archaeologists to verify the finding. What they saw was a lance point embedded between two ribs, demonstrating conclusively that ancient humans had killed the animals.

Disappearing New Mexico

Folsom Hotel Today - One Wonders if Malcom Bates is Home

The Folsom kills have been dated between 9,000 and 8,000 BC, essentially destroying Hrdlička's beliefs. Since the Folsom discovery, many other examples of hunting by archaic man in North America have been found.

View of the Many Closed Businesses on Main Street

George McJunkin was buried in the Dawson cemtery north of town.

Photo by Nancy Melin

Notes:

Mammoth remains containing arrow points were found near Clovis, New Mexico, at the Blackwater Draw site. These have been dated between 11,500 - 11,000 BCE. For many years, this was earliest evidence of Homo sapiens in North America.

Charcoal, found in a cave in the mountains north of Albuquerque (Sandia Man Cave), has been radiocarbon dated to about 25,000 years. However, because the soil had been disturbed, this dating is not universally accepted.

A more interesting find is the many footprints recently discovered at White Sands National Park. These have been rigorously studied and dated to 22,000-24,000 years BCE. There are footprints of adults and children. There are also prints of giant ground sloths, which may have been hunted there.

Ancient Foot Prints
at White Sands

La Cueva (Mora County)

From the south, take Exit 343 onto US-85 and head into Las Vegas. After about 2 miles, turn left onto seventh Street. This is NM-518. It will lead you past Storie Lake, a New Mexico State Park. Stay on 518 for about 25 miles and turn onto NM-442 at the intersection. The mill and store are about 125 yard east of NM-518.

From the northeast side of Las Vegas take Exit 364 and turn north onto NM-161. The highway intersects NM-518 after about 23 miles. Turn right onto 518. La Cueva is on the right, another 2 miles ahead.

Other places of interest that are reachable from this exit are Watrus, Tiptonville and Fort Union. Also, Loma Parda, an old bawdy town, is on the right side of NM-161, about eight miles from I-25. It is surrounded by the Wind River Ranch, now a new National Wildlife Refuge. Note: NM-161 goes north to different places on both sides of Watrus.

Vincenite Romero inhabited caves in the area and fished there during the 1830's. He named it La Cueva de los Pescaderos[52,53]. In English it's the cave of the fisher people. Romero also prospered through farming and was able to build several adobe buildings in the area. Today, no one seems to know where the caves are.

La Cueva, with its abundant supply of water, was well suited to growing wheat. In the 1860's, when Fort Union expanded, Romero built a mill at La Cueva and supplied flour to the Fort, as well as to the local people. The mill is no longer operational. Entering it is thought to be unsafe. However, the water wheel is clearly visible from the road, as is the raceway that brought water to it. Several mill stones are also found on the property.

Disappearing New Mexico

Mill Stone

Overshot Water Wheel

Adjacent to the mill is the Salmon Ranch store, which is locally famous. The Salmon Ranch grows raspberries and produces a variety of raspberry products, including an excellent jam, toppings, vinegar and several types of candy. From mid-August to mid-October, you may pick your own raspberries, but this is very weather dependent. See their web site (www.salmanraspberryranch.com) for store hours and more information.

About 500 feet further along on NM-442, on the right, is a dirt road that leads to the restored San Rafael Mission. The mission was built in the 1860's in French Gothic style.

The La Cueva Historic District was added to the National Register of Historic Sites in 1973.

San Rafael Mission

Loma Parda (Mora County)

From I-25, take exit 364 (19 miles northeast of Las Vegas) and turn north on NM-161. Proceed about 7 miles past the Wind River Ranch (now the Rio Mora National Wildlife Refuge) and turn right at the first dirt road. There is (was) a sign announcing Loma Parda. Continue downhill and cross the bridge over the Mora River. Loma Parda is ahead of you. Ben de Baca's old house is on the right.

Loma Parda[54-56], which is Spanish for brown hill, has had at least four lives. First it was a small, quiet farming community along the Mora River. When Fort Union moved in, about four miles to the northeast, things changed. Soldiers at Fort Union were looking for women, wine, and song. Loma Parda was quick to accommodate.

Today Loma Parda is almost abandoned. Its historic buildings may not survive much longer. Vandals have uprooted gravestones and thrown them into the Mora River. Buildings have collapsed or have been knocked down. Recently, the property has been surrounded, or taken over, by the Rio Mora National Wildlife Refuge. This may ultimately restrict access to the old buildings. In fact, NWR signs now surround many of the old buildings. Hurry if you want to visit Loma Parda. The old town may not be there much longer.

After Fort Union moved next door, Loma Parda became a bawdy town that serviced the boys from Fort Union. It was frequently called "Sodom on the Mora." A publication available at Fort Union often peddles the shady side of Loma Parda.

Julien Baca's Dance Hall – It Operated 27/7 with Wagon Service to Fort Union
The Courtyard Was Ringed with Cribs or Small Bedrooms

However, the village was typical of "boys' towns" all over.

In its heyday Loma Parda was rowdy. It had fights, shootings, and lynchings. "Loma Lightning" (actually brewed in Taos) flowed freely, and girls of the night

Disappearing New Mexico

were plentiful. Julian Baca's dance hall played music 24/7, while Toribio C. de Baca's wagons hauled soldiers to and from Fort Uion.

At various times Fort Union's commander declared Loma Parda off limits. That didn't deter the soldiers. Many were court marshaled for various offenses. One of the more colorful events involved a soldier who got so drunk he walked back to the fort without his clothes. He spent a considerable time in one of the Post's miserably hot jail cells.

After the Fort Union closed in 1891, Loma Parda returned to its peaceful old self. A schoolhouse was built, and Dora Ortiz Vasquez, schoolteacher from 1926-1927, lived on the second floor of the building. She described the community as delightful.

Adobe Building at the Entrance to Loma Parda

Inside Building to the Left

At that time, a church was across Main Street from the school. The church collapsed long ago. If you look among the rubble, you may still find a brown, weathered wooden cross, standing or lying among the stones. There was also a store/residence. The owner lived in the right side.

The ruins of the Dance Hall, the old school building, the store, and a stone corral are about all that remains. Note the courtyard to the rear of the dance hall in the photo on page 39.

Schoolhouse and Church

Sunflowers in Julian Baca's Dance Hall

One of Loma Parda's Two Cemeteries

Unfortunately, there has been significant vandalism of grave markers at the two cemeteries.

Loma Parda is changing. Since becoming National Wildlife Refuge several of the old buildings have been removed and have been replaced by modern pre-fab structures.

Watrous (Mora County)

From I-25, take Exit 364 (19 miles northeast of Las Vegas) and turn south on NM-161. One could also take Exit 366, turn south, and make a right turn onto 161. Watrous is ahead of you.

Watrous[57] is a small community of about 135 people. From 1821 until the railroads arrived, Watrus was an important point on the Santa Fe Trail. There, the Mountain and the Cimarron routes merged, before proceeding west toward Santa Fe. At that time, Watrous was named La Junta (the meeting or junction). The town was later renamed for Samuel Watrous, a merchant and landowner, who moved to New Mexico in 1835, and provided supplies for the travelers.

Although Watrous has many old and dilapidated buildings, one of the more interesting ones is found on 2nd Street, between Concord and Oliver. The building, which is back in the trees,

Disappearing New Mexico

has had many lives. At times it served as a Masonic Lodge for Fort Union soldiers, then a convent, and still later, it became a bordello.

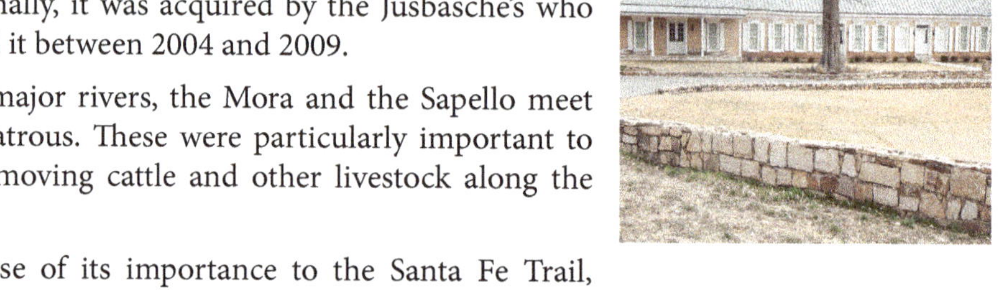

The Watrous House was built by Samuel Watrous in 1841. It was subsequently owned by three other families. Finally, it was acquired by the Jusbasche's who restored it between 2004 and 2009.

Two major rivers, the Mora and the Sapello meet near Watrous. These were particularly important to people moving cattle and other livestock along the trail.

Because of its importance to the Santa Fe Trail, Watrous (La Junta) has been designated a National Historic Landmark.

Tiptonville (Mora County)

Tiptonville can be reached from I-25 by taking Exit 366 and traveling toward Fort Union on NM-161. Tiptonville is about a mile from I-25. However, it is privately owned. You may drive through it and return to 161, but you won't see much.

Tiptonville[58] is on the way to Fort Union. The road past Tiptonville is part of the old Santa Fe Trail. Along the trail, several abandoned adobe buildings may be visible. After 0.7 miles, the trail dead ends at an east-west crossroad. Turn right and proceed about 300 feet to Hwy-161. There, turn left and go north to Fort Union or turn right for Watrous.

Ranch Buildings along the Way

More Adobe Buildings along the Road

Northeastern Counties

Fort Union (Mora County)

Fort Union is easily reached from I-25 by taking Exit 366 and traveling eight miles north on NM-161.

On route, about a mile past I-25, you pass Tiptonville, another ghost town.

Fort Union is huge, but weather has reduced many of its buildings to adobe corners and brick chimneys. A friend once called it the "Stonehenge of the Southwest". Indeed, there is a surreal look to the old fort[14,32,59-62].

Panaramic View of Fort Union (not including the Hospital and other buildings to the right)

In April 1851, Lt. Col. Edwin V. Sumner was ordered "to revise the whole system of defense" for the New Mexico territory. Among his first acts was to break up the scattered garrisons and relocate them in posts closer to the Indians. He also moved his headquarters and supply depot from Santa Fe, "that sink of vice and extravagance", to a site near the Mountain and Cimarron branches of the Santa Fe Trail. That is where he established Fort Union.

Mechanic's Corral where Wagons Were Serviced and Repaired

Disappearing New Mexico

The third fort, the one seen today, was abandoned in 1891 when the railroad replaced wagons on the Trail. In its heyday Fort Union had as many as 3,000 troops, and was the largest military site west of the Mississippi. It also housed many civilian contractors. Although officers were allowed to have wives, this was discouraged. Almost all wives on post had to perform services for the military, like doing laundry.

In addition to providing protection for wagons on the trail, Fort Union was the distribution point and repair center for military supplies west of the Mississippi. Wagons loaded with supplies would arrive at Fort Union and be unloaded. Their contents were then redistributed to some 50 other military posts across the west.

Many of the walls at Fort Union were made of adobe. Adobe requires frequent maintenance to counteract the effects of weather. For many years, Fort Union lay abandoned, without any maintenance. Local ranchers thought the walls a nuisance. Some even attempted to destroy the old buildings to protect their cattle. Fort Union Nation Monument was created on June 28, 1954.

Offices and Officer's Quarters

The post hospital treated the soldiers, and occasionally local residents. Official capacity was thirty-two. It could handle 128 in an emergecy.

The Post Hospital

Inside a Standard Officer's Quarters (left)

This stockade (right) could be really miserable in the hot New Mexican summers.

La Liendre (San Miguel County)

Take NM-104 east from Las Vegas about eight miles and turn south on NM-67 for about nine miles. The road is partially paved but is in bad repair. There are very steep drop-offs on the left. The view is spectacular, but please drive carefully. There is no guardrail.

In Spanish, La Liendre means "the nits". La Liendre was settled in the 1840's. It was once a stock raising community. It is in a beautiful setting on a bluff above the Gallinas River. It had a post office (closed in 1942), a store, a school, and a church. Little is left but crumbling stonewalls of buildings. It is likely that both the Depression and World War II contributed to the town's demise. The walls of the church are still

Disappearing New Mexico

recognizable, and there is another building with a partially collapsesd roof. One of these buildings appears to have been the schoolhouse and the other the general store.

Ruins of the Church at La Liendre

Collapsed Entrance to the Church

Remains of the Old Store

View of the Gallinas River from La Linedre

San Geronimo (San Miguel County)

As you approach Las Vegas on I-25 from the south, take Exit 343 to Grand Ave, turn right and immediately take another right onto the I-25 access road.

From the north, drive past the first two Las Vegas exits and take Exit 343, turn left onto Grand Ave. and then right onto the I-25 service road. Continuing on the service road until it intersects NM-283, turn right onto 283, go under the interstate and continue until you reach a fork in the road.

Keep left. San Geronimo is down the hill about a mile ahead of you. The drive is about 9.7 miles from the I-25 underpass.

San Geronimo[63] is a small, occupied community west of Las Vegas. It was established in the early 1830s. It is typical of other Mexican land grant villages that were also constructed of stone, adobe, and logs. Originally homes were built close together for protection from the Indians. The railroad brought a measure of prosperity to San Geronimo. Its sawmill produced the wooden ties needed for the tracks. Today very few families are left.

Disappearing New Mexico

Abandoned House in San Geronimo

View of the Cemetery

San Geronimo is listed on the National Register of Historic Places.

Encino (Torrance County)

From I-40, Encino can be reached turning onto US-285 at Clines Corner (Exit 218) and driving southeast for 29 miles.

From Santa Rosa, take US-54 southwest until it joins US-60/285 (about 38 miles). Bear right, get onto 285 and continue to Encino (17 miles).

From the junction of I-25 and US-60, drive east on US-60 for 87 miles and you are there.

Note: We find Encino, Vaughn and Yeso are best viewed in a single trip that starts here, and proceeds south.

Encino is the Spanish name for a scrubby oak, formerly common on the central plains of New Mexico. In 1905, the Atchison, Topeka and Santa Fe Railway announced plans to open a depot in Encino. The fact that Encino had a spring may have influenced that decision. In 1907 Encino's post office opened. Churches, a school, and a newspaper followed.

Encino must have once seen considerable commercial traffic due to the merger of two major highways, US-60 and US-285, plus a railroad depot. Several retail businesses were along the corridor, including a mercantile, a grocery, a laundry, a café, a CB radio shop, and a motel.

Old Grocery for Sale

Encino Motel Vewed from US-54 in 2013

The Railroad depot closed in 1965, hitting Encino's economy hard. Then the high school closed in 1982. Many of Encino's people have left. The population is now about 90. The old adobe buildings are slowly falling into ruin. Many of the building are for sale, but there seem to be few interested buyers.

Abandoned vehicles can be found in the fields in and around Encino.

Disappearing New Mexico

In recent years, windmills have become a populary means of generating electricity. The Encino area is currently home to a very large collection of wind farms.

Building for Sale (Old Restaurant?)

Colonias (Guadalupe County)

Six miles west of Santa Rosa take Exit 267 off from I-40 and turn north onto highway 379. Keep to the right at the three-way fork a mile up the road. Continue along Colonias Road for about 8-9 miles until you reach the community. The church is on the right.

San Jose Catholic Church is the centerpiece of Colonias[64], one of the oldest settlements on New Mexico's high eastern plains. Settled in the 1780s as Las Colonias, the community consisted of farmers and sheepherders. Colonias is located about 10 miles northwest of Santa Rosa on NM-279.

The San Jose Church holds historical value for the residents of Colonias, but also for high eastern plains of New Mexico. During the late 1990s the left tower of the Church collapsed, making the building unsafe. The current image was made in 2013 and shows the entire front of the Church, including the collapsed steeple on the left. The cracks on the right side are clearly visible (next page).

Residents and friends of Colonias are trying to raise money to restore this landmark, bur the diocese seems disinterested in funding the work, probacly due to relatively small population. As late as 2023, the church still needs repair.

Many other, older buildings are also in ruins.

Front View of San Jose Catholic Church

Remains of the Left Steeple

Cracks in the Right Steeple

Disappearing New Mexico

Dilia (Guadalupe County)

Dilia is 26 miles south of I-25 on US-84. It may also be reached by taking I-40 to Exit 291 and driving north for 15 miles.

Sacred Heart Catholic Church

Dilia[65] is on the road that connects Las Vegas and Santa Rosa. In previous times, a stagecoach ran between the two towns. The stage run took about ten hours. Dilia, being about halfway between the two, was a stop where fresh horses were taken on, passengers got to stretch their legs, and to get something to eat. US-84 has replaced the old trail.

Today the sixty-seven-mile trip between Las Vegas and Santa Rosa only takes about an hour. There is no need to stop. Except for Sacred Heart Catholic Church, the Maestas Lounge, and a few homes, there isn't much left of Dilia. The other businesses have closed.

The church is on west side of US-84, where CR-119 runs past it, on the way to Antone Chico. On the right side of 84 there is an interesting old hacienda that's worth a picture or two. There are also a few modern dwellings around the intersection.

A Store that Has Seen Better Days

Interesting Old Hacienda on Right Side of US-84

Maestas Lounge - Dilia

Disappearing New Mexico

Anton Chico (Guadalupe County)

Take Hwy-119 into Anton Chico, where it becomes Hwy-386. Turn right at the Rita M. Marquez Elementary School and follow San Jose Circle around the town.

Anton Chico[66] is a small community with substantial Hispanic roots. Today the population is about 188, but in 1890 roughly 900 people lived there. Then, it was the commercial center of eastern New Mexico. Since that time, the population has steadily declined.

San Jose Catholic Church

Anton Chico has the San Jose Catholic Church, an elementary school, a post office, and a library.

Once, there was a substantial retail establishment known as Abercrombie's (below - not related to the well known store in New York). The old building is still there, but the business is not.

The town hosts many modern structures, but there are also plenty that have a ghostly look.

Dilapidated Dwelling in Anton Chico

Cuervo (Guadalupe County)

Cuervo is on I-40, 18 miles east of Santa Rosa.

Cuervo[67-68] is a town divided. It began in 1901 when the railroad came through. Around 1910 land in the area was opened to cattle ranching. The town began to grow. Then, Route 66 came through and cut the town in two. However, the new highway brought service businesses that helped the town achieve a population of about 300 in the 1930s. At that point Cuervo had two schools, churches, hotels, doctors, and other businesses. But, by the 1940's the population had shrunk to less than 150.

Then, I-40 came through and truly cut the town in half. Cuervo couldn't prosper with that division. Today, about 50 people live around Cuervo, mostly on the south side of I-40 and on nearby ranches. The post office has closed and Cuervo is considered a ghost town.

A Boxcar Home with a More Conventional Home and a Church

Disappearing New Mexico

On the south side of the highway there is a Catholic Church that dates to World War I, the remains of a school constructed in the 1930s, a variety of old buildings in various states of decay, and a boxcar converted into a dwelling. There are more abandoned houses on the south side of I-40.

The Remains of a Route 66 Era Gas Station on the North Side of I-40

Abandoned Business in Cuervo, North of I-40

On the north side of I-40 there is an old, abandoned gas station, and a falling down Baptist Church. Cuervo Gas is further east on the frontage road.

If you are into old buildings, Cuervo may be your place.

Newkirk (Guadalupe)

Located along I-40 at Exit 300.

Newkirk[69] is another one of the towns that was decimated by the construction of Interstate-40. When Route 66 passed through, the road supported business for travelers. These included service stations, a motel, and a towing service.

The Remains of a Service Station on the South Side of I-40.
In the background trucks can be seen on the Interstate

An Abandoned Motel Is on the South Side of I-40

East of Newkirk, US 66 disappears and becomes a grassy field. Today, one lone gas station is still open.

Disappearing New Mexico

Abandoned Businesses North of I-40 (Wilkerson's On the Right)

Looking Into Wilkerson's Store

In 2010, the official population of Newkirk was seven.

San Jon (Quay County)

The next three towns can be reached either from the east (Texas) or from the west (New Mexico).

From New Mexico and east of Tucumcari, take Exit 335 from Interstate-40. The road is paved through San Jon. However, Quay County decided to stop maintaining "Old 66" because it got so little use. As a result, the road becomes dirt about 2.5 miles east of San Jan.

From the Texas side, take Exit 0 just before the state line. Then loop south under I-40 and turn right onto old "66". Route 66 is paved until it reaches the New Mexico state line.

San Jon[70] was founded in the early 1900's. Its initial growth was due to the railroad. When Route 66 came through, San Jon also became an important commercial location, particularly for motorists. Businesses, such as service stations, restaurants and motels were quite successful. However, I-40 effectively bypassed San Jon in 1981, forcing most of those businesses to close. The few that remain are on the north side of town and are centered around the interstate. The population of San Jon has shrunk to about 210.

Auto Parts on Route 66

Small Grocery Store Along the Road

Gasoline Station

Convenience Store/Garage

Disappearing New Mexico

Endee (Quay County)

Endee is about 14 miles east of San Jon and five miles west of Glenrio. Route 66 is not paved here.

There is very little left of Endee. A few abandoned houses remain, along with an old motel that offered modern restrooms.

A Motel from a Different Time

Driving south of Endee on SR-93 you will find a few abandoned houses, as well as the Endee Fire Station.

Abandoned House on SR-93

Glenrio (Quay County)

Continue on the dirt road until you reach pavement. This is the official state line.

Glenrio[71] was originally named Rock Island, when a railroad of that name stopped there. In 1908, the railroad company changed the town's name to Glenrio. By 1917, Glenrio was receiving motorists on the Ozark Trail, the forerunner of Route 66. On November 11, 1926, the road officially became US Route 66. On the Texas side, "Old 66" was, and is still paved. However, when I-40 opened in 1974, the old road saw little use. To save money, Quay County Commissioners voted to stop maintaining the eastern section of the old road. The pavement was removed.

Old Post Office

Abandoned Commercial Building in Glenrio

Disappearing New Mexico

The Last Motel In Texas?

Having Glenrio split across state lines produced some interesting business practices. Texas, with its lower tax on gasoline, had all the service stations. Conversely, because Deaf Smith County, Texas, was dry, the State Line Bar and Motel were in New Mexico. The railroad station was in Texas, but the post office, water tank and windmill were built in New Mexico.

Is the eastern part of Glenrio actually in Texas? Originally, the border was defined as the 103rd meridian. However, the 1859 survey mistakenly set the Texas border about three miles too far west. Interestingly, the New Mexico Senate passed a bill to fund a lawsuit with the U.S. Supreme Court to recover the land[72]. However, the bill was never signed into law. Glenrio isn't the real issue. This 800-900 square mile strip of land is in the oil rich Permian Basin. Tax revenue from it would have been significant.

In 2007, the Glenrio Historic District, which includes the Route 66 roadbed and 17 abandoned structures, were listed on the National Register of Historic Places.

Northeastern Counties

Vaughn (Guadalupe County)

From Encino, Vaughn can be reached by continuing southwest on US- 60/285 for 16 miles.

From Santa Rosa, take US-54 southwest until it joins US-60/285 (about 38 miles).

From the junction of I-25 and US-60, drive east on US-60 for 87 miles and you are there.

In the early part of the 20th century Vaughn[73] was established as a railroad town. The Southern Pacific Railroad was first, but later joined by the Atchison, Topeka and Santa Fe line in 1907. Soon, Vaughn had a two-story train station, a round house, and a Harvey House. In 1920 Vaughn's population was 888. The population has declined ever since, with 539 in 2000, 446 in 2010, and 397 in 2019.

The train depot is near the southern end town.

Station for the Atchison, Topeka & Santa Fe (ATSF) and El Paso & Southern Railroads

Many historic commercial buildings can still be found along Cedar Avenue (turn left, if coming into town from the north). There are many old buildings to see..

Disappearing New Mexico

The Peoples Store – General Merchandise

Appliance Store on Cedar Avenue

Hunton Bros Grocery

A Mercantile

Northeastern Counties

Duran (Torrance County)

Duran is easily reached from I-40 via US-285 (Exit 318 at Clines Corner) or US-54 (Exit 273 or 275 in Santa Rosa).

From Clines Corner take US-285 to NM-3 and turn right. Continue for 14 miles until you reach US-54 and Duran.

From Santa Rosa drive southwest on US-54 for 52 miles.

Duran[74] was a bustling railroad town in the era of steam engines. Trains stopped here to take on water. Later a repair depot was added. A town of about 300 grew up around the stop. With the coming of diesel engines, the rail stop was not needed, and even though US-54 runs through Duran, Interstate Highways took most of that traffic.

Today only about 35 people live in Duran. The town still has several interesting buildings, including the old general store and the San Juan Batista Catholic Church..

San Juan Batista Catholic Church

The Train Still Comes Through
- It Just Doesn't Stop

Disappearing New Mexico

The Front of the Old General Store Looks Good

In the Back, It's a Dumping Ground

Ancho, Lincoln County

Ancho is on NM-462, three miles from US-54. NM-462 is 19 miles north of Carrizozo and 54 miles south of the intersection of US-65 and US-60/286. It is easily reached from either I-40 or I-25.

Ancho has a train station that is not used. In fact, there never were any tracks near the station. The station was moved here and serves as a museum of sorts. The station is on private property and visitors are advised to view it from the road.

In the past[75-76] Phelps-Dodge operated a major brick factory here, but the remains of it are no longer visible.

Other features of Ancho include the schoolhouse that was built with Ancho brick. Several abandoned buildings and the Ancho cemetery are past the train station. A few people still live in and around Ancho.

Ancho Train Station -Front View

A Small Building East of the Train Station

Ancho Train Station - Side View from the Back

Disappearing New Mexico

Schoolhouse Built with Ancho Brick

Ancho brick was shipped to San Francisco to help rebuild the city after the earthquake of 1906.

Jicarilla (Lincoln County)

Jicarilla can be reached by taking A044 from Ancho. It's about 14 miles.

Placer mining for gold started in the Ancho-Jicarillo district as early as 1850, with Mexican-American prospectors hauling in water and washing the gravel in wooden pans. Anglo-American prospectors began working the area in 1880. By 1882 Jicarilla was a supply town, with a few stores and a post office, that also served as the assay office.

A few of the old buildings remain. The American Placer Company operated an unsuccessful dredge west of the post office, and a mill for processing ore was built somewhat later by the Wisconsin Milling and Smelting Company, again to no effect.

A Comercial Building in Jicarilla

A Residence in Jicarilla

Jicarilla[77] has been, and still is, a popular spot for finding placer gold. During the depression men moved into the gulches and mined and washed the gravels by hand as a means of survival. From 1933 to 1942 placer gold production was reported to be 1,814 Troy ounces (about $2.5 million in today's market). The log schoolhouse was built in 1907. The town, with its several remaining buildings, is some distance north of the school.

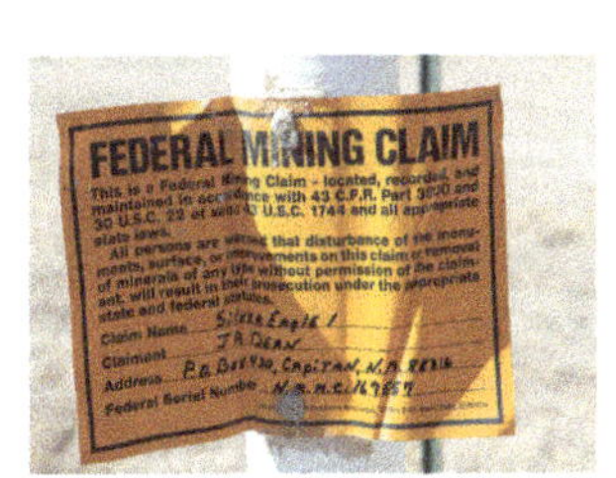

Federal Mining Claim

Jicarilla Schoolhouse

Disappearing New Mexico

White Oaks (Lincoln County)

In 1879, according to the story, a man named John Wilson spotted a vein of gold in the Jicarilla Mountains. It is likely that Wilson was running from the law because he sold his rights to the discovery to Jack Winters and Harry Baxter for couple of silver dollars, two ounces of gold dust and a pistol. Wilson then promptly disappeared.

As word of the strike spread, the town called White Oaks[78,79] began to grow in the nearby valley. Prospectors and merchants moved in. By 1890 White Oaks had a population of about 2,000, a bank, a post office, a newspaper, an opera house, several general stores, a school, a townhall, and a church. Like most western mining towns, it also had its share of saloons and brothels.

White Oaks Schoolhouse

Stairs to the Back Entrance

Cattle rustlers, horse thieves, and various other outlaws, including Billy the Kid and his gang, spent time in White Oaks. It is also said that Sherriff Pat Garrett came to White Oaks to buy lumber for Billy the Kid's scaffold on the day the Kid broke out of jail and killed two deputies.

Until they played out in the late 1890s, the mines near White Oaks produced $20,000,000 in gold and other minerals. At that time gold was valued at $19 per ounce (1.3-1.4 billion dollars in today's market). White Oaks' final economic failure was overpricing the right-of-way when the Railroad was considering laying tracks through town. The tracks ultimately went through Carrizozo, twelve miles away, and White Oaks truly began to die.

Currently, White Oaks has about 50 residents. The town is on the National Register of Historic Places. Many of its buildings are worth seeing. These include:

- The brick schoolhouse on the hill, which was built in 1895, is still in good shape. Desks and a piano can be seen through the window.

- The Gumm House above the school was built about 1891-1892. The Gumms ran a major lumber mill in the area.

- Hoyle House has been a landmark since it was built in 1893. It is reported to have cost $40,000. This house, later called Hoyle's Folly, was built for the girl of Hoyle's dreams. However, she met a cowboy on the train coming out, and got off in Tucumcari. She never arrived – thus its Hoyle's Folly.

Hoyle's Folly

The Gumm House

Disappearing New Mexico

- The Treat House was one of the few early buildings that had piped in water.
- The "No Scum Allowed Saloon" is a popular watering hole.

Gold mine tours can still be arranged by calling 565-648-4146.

No Scum Allowed Saloon

James Bell Grave - Terry Maznio Photo

James Bell was one of two deputies killed during "Billy the Kid's" escape from jail in Lincon. He is buried in the Cedarvale Cemetery about 2.0 miles southwest of White Oaks, on CR-349.

Fort Stanton (Lincoln County)

From I-25 in the west, take U-S-60/US-380 to Carrizozo.

From I-40 in the north, take 54/285 through Vaughn; continue on US-54 to Carrizozo; then go east through Capitan (20 miles) and turn south onto NM-220 to reach Fort Stanton (another 4.3 miles).

In addition to Fort Stanton proper, two other local areas may be of interest.

The Smokey Bear Historical Park is in Capitan. A badly burned black bear cub was found clinging to a tree in the Lincoln Forest. The cub was taken to Santa Fe and nursed back to health. Smokey the Bear has become an icon for forest fire awareness.

In 1855, the U.S. Army established Fort Stanton[80] as an Infantry and Cavalry post in the east-central New Mexico Territory. It was to protect settlers in the region. The fort played a significant role in dealing with Mescalero Apaches confined in a nearby reservation. It also became a major player in the Lincoln Wars. In 1861 Confederate forces briefly occupied the fort at the beginning of the American Civil War.

Officer's Quarters

Other Buildings at Fort Stanton

In 1899, President William McKinley transferred Fort Stanton from the War Department to the Marine Hospital Service, where it became the first federal tuberculosis sanitorium. The fort hosted about 5,000 sailor patients between 1889 and 1953, About 1,500 are buried in the adjacent cemetery.

Disappearing New Mexico

The Catholic Chapel at Fort Stanton

During the 1940s the fort was also used as an internment camp for German and Japanese prisoners of war. There were a few attempts to escape, but the remoteness of the area made escape futile. The hospital closed in 1953.

In 2008, Governor Bill Richardson announced plans to make Fort Stanton a living history site. It is now Fort Stanton State Monument.

Merchant Marine Military Cemetery and State Veterans Cemetery is shown below.

Merchant Marine Military Cemetery and State Veterans Cemetery

The Fort Stanton-Snow River Cave National Conservation Area (NCA) is located on fort property. The cave, which extends for over 42 miles, is one of the larger cave systems in the US. However, to protect the resident bats from the White Nose Syndrome, access to the cave is limited to researchers with Special Recreation Permits. The cave system is managed by the Bureau of Land Management (BLM).

Southeastern Counties

Lincoln (Lincoln County)

From Fort Stanton, return to US-380; turn right and drive for nine miles.

The stories of William Henry McCarty[81-83] (aka Billy the Kid) and the Lincoln Wars are well known, but they seem to vary considerably, depending on who is telling them. Our version may differ from others.

It should be noted that when the U.S. first occupied New Mexico, Lincoln County was enormous. It was larger than the state of South Carolina.

The Lincoln War story starts with Lawrence Murphy, an Irishmen, and Emil Fritz, a German.[27, 34] The pair established a store at Stanton, and profited from contracts to supply beef, vegetables, and other goods to Fort Stanton. It also supplied the local Mescalero-Apache Reservation Agency. One of Murphy and Fritz's schemes was to sell land to farmers and ranchers, many of whom were unable make payments. The pair would then foreclose on the land, taking land, cattle, and crops. The pair also developed contacts with politicians in the Santa Fe Ring, a group who protected other special interests. In 1868, Murphy hired James Dolan, who had mustered out at Fort Stanton. Fritz, after being diagnosed with a kidney disease, returned to Germany. He died on June 26, 1874.

Torreon (a hideout during Indian Raids)

In May of 1873, Dolan attempted to shoot and kill James Randlett, a Captain at Fort Stanton. In September of that year, L.G. Murphy & Co. was evicted from Fort Stanton. This was partially due to the confrontation with Randlett, but also due to accusations of price gouging. Murphey and Dolan moved to Lincoln where they opened "Murphy & Dolan Mercantile and Banking", known as "The House". The contract with Fort Stanton continued.

The business rapidly monopolized the county's trade, controlling prices and making huge profits. The business had many allies, including local law enforcement, as well as important political figures in Santa Fe. Small farmers, however, were not happy because they were forced to pay high prices for merchandise and to accept low prices for items they sold. In addition to high prices, "the House" loaned money to ranchers at high interest rates. Due to cattle rustling sponsored by "the House", ranchers frequently couldn't keep up with the payments. "The House".

Disappearing New Mexico

would then foreclose on their land and seize their cattle. Later in the summer, a lawyer named Alexander McSween and John Tunstall, a wealthy 24-year old English cattleman, set up a rival business named H.H. Tunstall & Company. Tunstall's business was rapidly putting a dent the House's business. In response, Dolan and Riley used hired guns like the Jesse Evans gang and the Seven Rivers Warriors to steal Tunstall's cattle. Tunstall responded by hiring his people to protect his property. Dolan, upset with losing business, attempted to goad Tunstall into a gun fight. Tunstall refused.

McCarty ("Billy the Kid") originally worked at Sheriff Brady's ranch, while supplementing his income with rustling. Dick Brewer, Tunstall's foreman, caught McCarty stealing horses and had him thrown into jail. Tunstall visited McCarty in jail and was sufficiently impressed to offer McCarty a job. The job included a horse, a Winchester rifle, and a saddle, creating a lasting bond between the two. McCarty's devotion to Tunstall caught on with others at the ranch.

The trigger for the Lincoln County War was a dispute over Emil Fritz's insurance policy. McSween, the executor, refused to turn over the money to Dolan without reviewing his claim. Dolan used his allies to seize McSween's and Tunstall's assets, the latter being included because of the partnership in H.H. Tunstall & Company. Dolan's primary interest was eliminating the competition.

On February 18, 1878, Sheriff Brady formed a posse to seize Tunstall's livestock. When they arrived at the ranch, they realized Tunstall was on his way to Lincoln. Several men were dispatched to catch up with him. They found him in a canyon near Glenroe. Most of the party fled, but Tunstall stayed with the horses, possibly to negotiate. However, the posse came in shooting. Tunstall was shot both the chest and the head. He was killed.

McCarty and Brewer filed affidavits with "Squire" John Wilson, and the judge issued warrants for the men responsible. Constable Martinez deputized McCarty and Fred Waite to help serve the warrants, but when the men arrived at Dolan's store, Sheriff Brady refused to acknowledge the warrants and arrested the three men trying to serve them. All three were ultimately freed, but they were determined to get revenge. A group of fourteen men calling themselves "Regulators"rode out of Lincoln with warrants, determined to deliver justice.

On March 6, 1878, the Regulators caught up with three of the men. They planned to return them to Lincoln, but not believing the three would receive justice, the Regulators finally shot them.

Plank Sidewalk in Lincoln

In response to this, Sheriff Brady called on Attorney General Tomas Catron for help. Catron was a member of the Santa Fe Gang who controlled politics and law throughout the territory. He also had a vested financial interest in eliminating Tunstall and McSween. Catron had Governor Samuel Axtell travel to Lincoln and remove the judge who issued the warrants and invalidate them. He also revoked Widenmann's status a deputy marshal. This left Sheriff Brady as the only official law in Lincoln. Brady promptly issued warrants for McSween and the Regulators.

On April 1, 1878, the Regulators hid in a corral behind Tunstall's store. They ambushed Sheriff Brady and his deputies on the way to arrest Alexander McSween.

Brady was hit at least a dozen times. McCarty recovered the Winchester Brady had taken from him earlier. On April 4th, the Regulators caught up with Buckshot Roberts and killed him. Dick Brewer, a Regulator, was fatally wounded in the battle. The Regulators elected Frank McNab as their new captain, but he was shot and killed at Fritz's ranch. Attacks continued throughout May and June.

Dolan asked the Colonel at Fort Stanton for help. Even though it was illegal for the army to be used against American citizens, the military arrived with a Gatling gun and a howitzer, surrounded the town, and separated small groups of Regulators from those stuck in houses. Dolan's men fired on the Regulators, getting them to return fire so the soldiers would get involved. McCarty was trapped in McSween's house along with him and his wife, several Regulators and a dozen Mexican cowboys.

While the troops from Fort Stanton watched on July 19, Dolan's people set fire to McSween's house. Women and children were allowed to leave, but everyone else was to be shot. Jim French and McCarty then devised a plan to shoot their way out to create a diversion for the unarmed men. French and McCarty then led a charge out the back door. Dolan's people fired on them. A total of three men were gunned

Disappearing New Mexico

down, including McSween. With two exceptions, the Regulators escaped. Dolan and his men celebrated by getting drunk and looting Tunstall's store. The Battle of Lincoln ended the Lincoln County War.

After the War

McCarty and three other survivors of the "Battle of Lincoln" were near the Mescalero Indian Agency when the agency bookkeeper, Morris Bernstein, was murdered on August 5, 1878. McCarty and friends were indicted for the murder, despite evidence that Bernstein was killed by a local constable. All indictments, except McCarty's, were later quashed.

Frank Angel, a federal investigator, wrote to President Rutherford B. Hayes and criticized the governor's role in the war. Angel concluded that Tunstall was murdered in "cold blood" by Brady's posse. His letter to Secretary of the Interior included the words: "The Territorial Government has more corruption, fraud, mismanagement, plots, and murder than any other ... in the history of the United States...".

Governor Axtell was shortly replaced by Lew Wallace, a well-known civil war general. Wallace immediately called for a halt to the violence and granted amnesty to all but one of those involved.

On October 5, 1878, U.S. Marshal John Sherman informed newly appointed Territorial Governor Lew Wallace that he held warrants for several men, including McCarty. However, he claimed to be unable to execute them due to conditions in Lincoln County. Wallace issued an amnesty proclamation on November 13, 1878, which pardoned anyone involved in the Lincoln County War since Tunstall's murder. It specifically excluded persons who had been convicted of or indicted for a crime, therefore excluding McCarty.

McCarty met secretly with Wallace on March 17, 1879, where the governor asked him to surrender voluntarily and testify before a grand jury investigating the murders of Tunstall and Chapman. The testimony was to be for a full pardon.

In April, over 200 criminal inditements were made against Dolan and his men. Many of Dolan's men took advantage of the offer of amnesty. The courts acquitted everyone involved. Dolan later acquired Tunstall's property. Tunstall's family was left with nothing.

On February 18, 1879, McCarty and Tom O'Folliard were in Lincoln, where they watched as attorney Huston Chapman was shot and his corpse set on fire. Bystanders claimed the pair were innocent but were forced to witness the murder.

McCarty wrote to Governor Wallace on March 13, 1879, offering to provide information on the Chapman murder in exchange for amnesty. Governor Wallace replied, agreeing to a secret meeting to discuss the situation. McCarty met with Wallace in Lincoln on March 17, 1879. Wallace promised McCarty protection from his enemies and clemency if he would offer his testimony to a grand jury. The Governor added, "to remove all suspicion of understanding, I think it better to put the arresting party in charge of Sheriff Kimball of Lincoln County who "shall be instructed to see that no violence is used."

McCarty wrote back, agreeing to testify and confirming Wallace's proposal for his arrest and detention in a local jail. On March 21, McCarty let himself be captured by a posse led by Kimball. As agreed, McCarty provided a statement about Chapman's murder and testified in court.

However, after McCarty's testimony, the local district attorney refused to set him free. Still in custody several weeks later, McCarty began to suspect Wallace had used subterfuge and would never grant him amnesty. McCarty escaped from the Lincoln County jail on June 17, 1879.

McCarty avoided further violence until January 10, 1880, when he shot and killed Joe Grant, a newcomer to the area, at Hargrove's Saloon in Fort Sumner. McCarty had been warned that Grant intended to kill him. He walked up to Grant and asked to examine his revolver. Before returning the pistol, McCarty positioned the cylinder so the hammer would fall on an empty chamber. Grant suddenly pointed his pistol at McCarty's face and pulled the trigger. When it failed to fire, McCarty drew his own weapon and shot Grant in the head.

Later in 1880, McCarty formed a friendship with a rancher named Jim Greathouse, who introduced him to Dave Rudabaugh. On November 29, 1880, McCarty, Rudabaugh, and Billy Wilson ran from a posse led by a sheriff's deputy. Cornered at Greathouse's ranch, McCarty told the posse they were holding Greathouse as a hostage. McCarty accepted the deputy's offer to exchange places with Greathouse. However, Deputy Carlysle later attempted to escape, and was shot three times and killed. The shootout ended in a standoff, with the posse withdrawing.

Shortly after the Greathouse encounter, McCarty, Rudabaugh, Wilson, O'Folliard, Charlie Bowdre, and Tom Pickett rode into Fort Sumner. But a posse led by Pat Garrett was waiting for them. The posse opened fire, killing O'Folliard; the rest of the outlaws escaped.

Disappearing New Mexico

On December 13, 1880, Lew Wallace posted a new $500 bounty for McCarty's capture. Pat Garrett continued his search for McCarty, and on December 23, following the siege in which Bowdre was killed, Garrett and his posse captured McCarty, Pickett, Rudabaugh, and Wilson. The prisoners were taken to Fort Sumner and then to Las Vegas. The party proceeded to Santa Fe the next day.

In Santa Fe and over a period of three months, McCarty sent Governor Wallace four letters, but the governor refused to intervene. McCarty's trial for the murder of Sherriff William Brady was scheduled to take place in Mesilla, not Lincoln. Due to the large number of McCarty's friends there, the Santa Fe lawyers didn't think they could find an impartial jury in Lincoln. The trial was set for April 1881. McCarty's lawyer was Albert Fountain, who was appointed at the last minute and had little time to prepare for the defense.

After two days of testimony, McCarty was found guilty of Brady's murder. This was the only conviction secured against any of the participants in the Lincoln County War. On April 13, Judge Warren Bristol sentenced McCarty to "hang, hang, hang". His execution was scheduled for May 13, 1881.

Lincoln County Courthouse - Billy the Kid Escaped from Here

McCarty was moved to Lincoln. He was held on the top floor of the courthouse. On the evening of April 28, 1881, while Garrett was in White Oaks buying lumber for the hangman's scaffold, Deputy Bob Olinger took five prisoners across the street for a meal. Deputy James Bell was left alone with McCarty. The prisoner asked to use the privy.

On their return, McCarty, hid around a blind corner, slipped out of his handcuffs, and beat Bell with the loose end of the cuffs. During the scuffle, McCarty grabbed Bell's revolver and fatally shot him as Bell tried to get away.

With his legs shackled, McCarty broke into Garrett's office and took a loaded shotgun. He waited at the window for Olinger to respond to the gunshot and called "Look up, old boy". When Olinger looked up, MaCarty killed him. McCarty freed himself from the leg irons, obtained a horse and rode out of town.

Almost three months after his escape, Garrett responded to rumors that McCarty was in the vicinity of Fort Sumner. Garrett and two deputies left Lincoln on July 14, 1881. There, Garrett spent time questioning Pete Maxwell, the son of Lucien Maxwell and a friend of McCarty's. There are several versions of what happened at Maxwell's house, leading to controversy about what really happened.

Pat Garrett's Version

Around midnight, Garrett sat in Maxwell's darkened bedroom. McCarty un-epectedly entered, but because of poor lighting, failed to recognize Garrett. Drawing his revolver and backing away, McCarty asked in Spanish, "Who is it? Who is it?". Recognizing McCarty's voice, Garrett drew his revolver and fired twice. The first bullet struck McCarty in the chest just above his heart, and the second missed. Garrett's account leaves it unclear whether McCarty was killed instantly or took some time to die.

A few hours after the shooting, a local justice of the peace assembled a coroner's jury of six people. The jury members interviewed Maxwell and Garrett. McCarty's body and the location of the shooting were examined. The jury certified the body was McCarty's. McCarty was given a wake by candlelight; he was buried the next day and his grave was denoted with a wooden marker.

A Different Version of the story

An alternate version had McCarty in bed with a young woman who happened to be pregnant, perhaps with his child. Somebody was clearly shot, but there is no mention of a coroner's jury. The story indicates that Garrett and the woman were the only ones to see the body, with her preparing it for burial. Since Garrett was a

Disappearing New Mexico

friend of McCarty's and only he and the woman saw the body, there has always been a question about what really happened.

In the Aftermath

After McCarty's killing, Garrett went to Santa Fe to collect the $500 reward. However, William G. Ritch, the acting governor, refused to pay. Over the next few weeks, residents of Las Vegas, Mesilla, Santa Fe, White Oaks and other cities raised over $7,000 in reward money for Garrett.

Burial

The day after the shooting, McCarty was buried at the Fort Sumner cemetery (about three miles east of town). His two companions, Tom O'Folliard and Charlie Bowdre are also buried there. The original location of the graves is uncertain because flooding scattered the grave markers and bones.

The Pecos River, which long had a reputation for being wild, flooded the area where Maxwell's house stood. The flood destroyed the house, so we have no photographs of it.

In the early 1930's, Charles Foor gave tours of the graveyard and saved his tip money. He later paid for a single marble tombstone for the three outlaws. The epitaph reads "Pals". A year later the burial plot was enclosed by a nine-foot-high chain-link fence to protect the headstone from souvenir hunters.

James Noah Warner (1892-1962), a Colorado stonecutter, decided that Billy the Kid needed his own gravestone. He carved one with two crossed pistols and 21 notches for the men that Billy supposedly killed. The stone included the epitaphs: "Truth and History" and "The Boy Bandit King. He Died As He Had Lived." Warner put the stone in his car and drove 400 miles from Salida, Colorado to Fort Sumner. On March 23, 1940, the new stone was placed at the foot of Billy's grave.

This headstone lasted barely ten years. On July 6, 1950, it was stolen, shortly after Ollie P. Roberts came to Santa Fe claiming to be McCarty. The original stone was missing for 25 years, until two tourists claimed seeing it in a pasture near Granbury, Texas. It was there, hidden under a boxcar. The stone was returned to the Fort Sumner on June 19, 1976. This time it was anchored to a concrete base and secured by a steel cap.

In February 1981 a truck driver having the CB handle "Billy the Kid" used a crowbar to pry the stone loose. He then drove it to Huntington Beach, California.

He was apprehended and the gravestone was returned. This time the stone was shackled in iron and the whole cemetery plot was enclosed in a steel cage.

Yeso (De Baca County)

From I-40 at Santa Rosa, take US-54 south. After 42 miles turn west onto US-60. Yeso is 22 miles from the junction just southeast of Vaughn.

From Vaughn go east on US-60, being careful to stay to the right where US-54 and US-60 split.

Yeso[84,85] is an unusual ghost town, about 20 miles west of Fort Sumner. US-60 goes right through it. The highway is lined with many buildings, but almost none are occupied. Most are in ruins. One exception is the prefab post office that replaced the old one shown in earlier ghost town books and web sites. The post office serves the few people that still live in the area. The current population is about 40.

Yeso means "gypsum" in Spanish. The town came into being in 1906, when the Atchison, Topeka and Santa Fe Railway came through the area. Although water from Yeso creek was not fit for drinking, there was accessible groundwater for livestock and locomotives traveling the Belen Cutoff. Yeso also became a trading center for ranchers. Its post office opened in 1909. Many of original settlers moved away when it became clear that the land was not good for farming, being good only for sheepherding and grazing.

After World War II, when diesel engines were introduced, the trains no longer stopped for water. The effect on the Yeso's economy was disastrous. In the mid-1960's, the local school closed. Almost everyone left, many moving to Fort Sumner to the east.

Along US-60, an array of decaying buildings remains, including the Frontier "Museum", what's left of the Super Service Garage, a mercantile, and a row of stone buildings that suggest a motel. Off the highway there are several abandoned residential structures and a church. For those interested in photographing ghost towns Yeso is amazing. However, many of the old buildings that were present ten years ago are now gone. Hurry if you want to see what does remain of Yeso.

Disappearing New Mexico

The Remains of Yeso's Old Service Station

Old Museum/Antique Store in Yeso

Abandoned Antique Store

Remains of a Stone Structure Along US-60

One of Many Abandoned Dwellings North of US-60

Disappearing New Mexico

What's Left of Yeso's One-room Schoolhouse

Organ (Doña Ana County)

Organ is on US-70, about 13 miles north of its intersection with I-25 near Las Cruces.

Organ was once a significant mining town, producing lead, copper, and silver. However, today it is largely a trailer town, with a few permanent structures scattered among the streets. In 2010 the population was 323. It is difficult to find many of the the old buildings among the trailers. An exception is the old schoolhouse at the corner of "B" Street and Third. According to last report, the famous Bentley Store is now a private residence.

The old schoolhouse does have a new metal roof.

Old Stone Schoolhouse at Organ

Dripping Springs (Doña Ana, County)

In Las Cruces, take Exit 1 east from I-25.

The spectacular Organ Mountains separate Las Cruces from the White Sands Missile Range. Here, there are rugged peaks, beautiful fields, mountain flowers, and desert cacti. High in the mountain lies the Dripping Springs Natural Area, a Bureau of Land Management property. Dripping Springs contains offers wonderful trails, ruins from the past, and stories of past inhabitants[86-87].

Eugene Van Patten, a New Yorker, came to the Las Cruces area in 1857. In the late 1800s he decided to build a resort in the Organ Mountains, some 6,000 feet above the valley floor. By 1906, the resort had grown to thirty-two rooms, and a stage-coach brought customers from Las Cruces. By 1917, Van Patten, who was bankrupt, sold the resort to Dr. Nathan Boyd. Boyd intended to use the resort for "altitude therapy", which was used to treat tuberculosis at the time.

Boyd built his sanatorium near the site Van Patten had used for his resort. In

Disappearing New Mexico

1922 Dr. Boyd sold the property to Dr. Sexton, a Las Cruces physician, who continued to operate the sanitorium. By World War II there were pharmaceutical remedies for tuberculosis and Dripping Springs fell into disuse.

Front View of Van Patten's Hotel - The Walls are Two Feet Thick

Side View of the Hotel - left

A Second Hotel Building - right

Boyd's Sanatorium

View of Organ Mountains from the Trail

People driving east on I-25 toward Las Vegas will see a large rocky peak dominating the landscape to the north. Locals know it as Hermit's Peak. In the Dripping Springs Natural Area there is a cave below the visitors' center. It is known as Hermit's Cave. The same hermit also lived there later.

The Hermit's Cave

The story of the Hermit is at best, uncertain. Perhaps his name isn't even known. Various writings call him Giovanni Maria Augustani or Agostini-Justinianii. Most accounts say he was the son of a nobleman from the Tuscan region of Italy. One version of the story has him entering seminary school, but being seduced by a dark-eyed beauty. Another says he left over disagreements about church policy. A third version had him killing a man.

In any event, the Hermit left Italy in 1827, vowing never to accept holy orders and to live his life in solitude. For about ten years he wandered through Spain and other parts of Europe. In 1838 he sailed to South America where he traveled and lived in Venezuela, Brazil, Paraguay, Argentina, and Peru. Eventually, he crossed into Cen-

Disappearing New Mexico

tral America and Mexico. In Mexico, the then anti-clerical government expelled him. From Mexico he sailed to Cuba and then to Quebec. Finally, he moved south and traveled in the U.S.

At the age of 62, the Hermit joined a wagon train traveling the Santa Fe Trail from Kansas to New Mexico. He walked the entire 550 miles. For a short time, he lived in Romeroville, New Mexico, but then he moved to Cerro Tecolote. This mountain, now known as Hermits Peak, is northwest of Las Vegas. In that area he got to know Penitentes who believed in his healing powers. To this day they still honor him at Easter.

In 1867, Agostini walked 250 miles to Mesilla to seek legal advice from the well-known lawyer, Albert Fountain. No one knows what was discussed. From Mesilla he walked another 530 miles to San Antonio, Texas. Later he walked another 500 miles, back to a cave in Juarez, Mexico.

The Hermit's Cave

In 1869, he returned to Old Mesilla Plaza, where he spent time visiting the Barela family. He told them about *"La Cueva"* and his plans to move there. The Barelas and others warned him of the dangers of living alone in such a remote place. In response he said "I shall make a fire in front of my cave every Friday evening while I'm still alive. If the fire fails to appear, it will be because I have been killed. I shall bless you daily in my prayers."

On Friday, April 17, 1869, the fire didn't appear. Antonio Garcia led a group of people to the cave, where they found the Hermit lying face down with a knife in his back. He is buried in the Mesilla Cemetery. The inscription on his tombstone is in Spanish and reads "John Mary Justiniani, Hermit of the Old and New World."

Mesilla (Doña Ana County)

Go west on I-10 about 3.1 miles from the junction I-25. Turn left on Hwy-28 and proceede to Boutz Road and turn left. Mesilla Plaza is two blocks ahead; Calle De Guadalupe runs beside it. The Billy the Kid Gift shop is at the intersection of Guadalupe and Calle De Parian. The Fountain Theater is on Guadalupe in the next block.

This is a good place to spend an evening. There is much to see, much to do, and good food to eat.

McCarty's trial for murder took place in Mesilla. At that time Mesilla was part of Lincoln County. The old courthouse is now a gift shop.

McCarty's attorney was Albert Fountain, the well known lawyer, originally from Texas. The Fountain family was into the arts. Three theaters were actually started by them.

Two things may have affected Fountain's defense of McCarty:

1) Fountain was very opposed to lawlessness, cattle rustling in particular.

2) He was appointed to be McCarty's lawyer with very little time to prepare.

Courthouse Where Billy the Kid Was
Sentanced to Hang

The Fountain Theater

Disappearing New Mexico

The trial of McCarty for killing Sheriff William Brady began on April 8th with the selection of jurors. A day later those jurors found Billy guilty of first-degree murder, which carried a death sentence.

On April 13 Judge Warren Bristol sentenced McCarty to "hang! hang! hang!" in Lincoln a month later. During the trial McCarty did not testify in his own defense. In fact, Albert Fountain called no witnesses. McCarty's defense was only what Fountain told the jury on his behalf. It would appear Fountain gave McCarty less than a good defense.

McCarty probably had reasonable grounds for appeal, but no appeal was made. There was no transcript of the trial. The rule at the time being that if a case was not going to be appealed, the court did not need to pay for a formal transcript.

Mogollon (Catron County)

Take US-180 north from Silver City, drive past Buckhorn, Pleasanton and Glenwood; turn right onto NM-159 (about 66 miles). Proceed on 159 for 9 miles to Mogollon. Be warned that NM-159 is narrow in spots and traverses some very steep terrain. Also note that in 2013 the road was severely damaged by heavy rains and was not passable.

US-180 goes so close to the Arizona border our cell phones switched time zones.

In 1909 Mogollon[88-92] had a population of 2,000. Fire and flood have always plagued the town. Mogollon was once a major center of gold and silver mining. Remoteness and the rugged mountain terrain combined to make Mogollon a wild place. Currently, almost no one lives in Mogollon.

After World War II, Mogollon shrank as the demand for gold waned. Today few people live there. Food and lodging are available and there is hope that mining may be successful again. Mogollon is on the National Register of Historic Places.

The J.P. Holland General Store is a recognized landmark. The Mogollon Theater and the general store which are also along Bursum Road are recognized buildings. There is a museum on the south side of the Bursum Road. Not too long ago, test drillings were made to determine the economic feasibility of resuming gold mining.

J.P. Holland General Store

Disappearing New Mexico

Mogollon Theatre

Mogollon General Store

An interesting collection of old cars and gas pumps can be found on the north side of the road. The old mining area is uphill from the town.

When Did You Last See a Gas Price Like 21.9 Cents/Gallon?

Disappearing New Mexico

Magdalena (Socorro County)

From I-25 take US-60 through Socorro to Magdalena. It's about 27 miles. Magdalena can be the starting point for several ghost towns, but take the time to look around here.

Magdalena[93] began with the mines in Kelley, about two miles south on Kelley Road. Responding to the mines, the Santa Fe Railroad built a branch from Socorro to the new town of Magdalena in 1885.

The railroad made Magdalena. It became a railhead for shipping cattle. Ranchers in western New Mexico and eastern Arizona drove their cattle along the "Beefsteak Trail" to Magdalena, where they were loaded onto railcars and shipped to market. The cattle made about ten miles a day; sheep typically did five miles.

Magdalena was booming. Everybody, from miners to merchants was making money. In 1886 Magdalena had a church, a school, a bookstore, several saloons, and many other businesses.

Railroad Station in Magdalena - Now the Library

At the end of the trail, the cowboys tended to get a bit drunk and rowdy. They also visited ladies of the night. It was also common to race along Main Street while shooting their guns in the air. In her book, *"No Place for a Lady"*, Agnes Cleaveland says her mother asked the hotel attendant for a room that was not over the bar. She wasn't interested in bullets coming through the floor.

Magdalena's Hall Hotel - It Now Has Apartments for Rent

However, there was one group of cowboys who never got rowdy. For one year, Butch Cassidy was foreman of a ranch on the west side of New Mexico. Since the law was looking for him, he couldn't very well go to the jail to bail his boys out. When Cassidy was finally recognized, he told the rancher he had to be moving on.

By 1897, Magdalena was shipping wool to eastern markets. By the next year Magdalena wool was stored in warehouses until it was auctioned and shipped as far away as Boston. Later the Charles Ilfeld Company warehouse was built near the railroad terminal. Ilfeld sold supplies on credit and the ranchers paid the bills when the cattle or sheep were sold.

Disappearing New Mexico

Magdalena is not what it used to be. The population has shrunk to about 650. The magnificent Hall Hotel is now apartments, and the bank serves ice cream. But Magdalena is still worth a visit and a few photographs. It is also a starting point for trips to Kelley and to Riley.

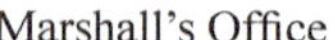

Marshall's Office

Old Bank of Magdalena Building

The Hall Hotel, with its walls three bricks thick, opened in 1917. By 1919 Magdalena had both a grade school and a high school. In 1929, when the Great Depression hit, the Bank of Magdalena failed. The following year the combination of drought and a saturated cattle market compounded the problems. To make matters worse, the government wool warehouse in Albuquerque offered cut rates to sheepmen. Ranchers loaded their sheep onto trucks and drove there. Trucks had also replaced cattle drives on the "Beefsteak Trail."

Kelly (Socorro County)

Take US-60 west from I-25 at Socorro and drive for 26 miles to the outskirts of Magdalena. Turn left onto Kelly Road. Drive 2 miles and keep to the left at the fork. Continue on the unpaved road for anther 1.7 miles and you are at Kelly.

J. S. Hutchason, "Old Hutch," discovered lead outcroppings in the Magdalena Mountains in the spring of 1866, a discovery that started the Magdalena Mining District[94,95]. Back then the ore was smelted locally in adobe furnaces and the metal hauled by ox team to Kansas City.

Around about 1879 prospectors attracted to the area, laid out a town on the west slope of the Magdalena Mountains. They named it Kelly. At the turn of the century, the lead and silver deposits were nearly exhausted, and the town was beginning to die. However, the mining at Kelly produced a greenish waste rock. Cory T. Brown of Socorro had some waste analyzed. It turned out to be smithsonite, a mineral, rich in zinc carbonate. The discovery of zinc gave Kelly a fresh breath of life. The Graphic Mine was sold to the Sherwin Williams Paint Company and the Kelly Mine to Tri-Bullion.

Kelly boomed with the profits from smithsonite as it became the state's leading producer of zinc. Kelly ultimately had two schools, three churches, and a moving picture house. By 1931 the smithsonite deposits were also exhausted. Gradually, mining throughout the district began to decrease. Once again, Kelly began to die.

Remains of the old town include the white-fronted Catholic Church, a few adobe and rock ruins, and the Kelly cemetery - all found along the dirt road leading up the hill.

Disappearing New Mexico

Headframe and Tipple, Tri-Bullion Mine
The Mine Is About 1,000 feet deep and Contains 31 Miles of Tunnel

Roasters, Tipple and Headframe
Tri-Bullion Mine

St. John the Baptist Catholic Church at Kelly

Mine equipment, tailings, roasting ovens, the tipple, the huge steel headframe, and other mine buildings are further up the road. The headframe is imposing because of its size. The elevator shaft is nearly 1,000 feet deep, leading to about 31 miles of tunnel.

Today, no one lives in Kelly.

Riley (Socorro County)

Take US-60 west from Socorro to Magdalena, then Farm Road 354 north from Magdalena. The signed 30-mile dirt road begins between the train station (library) and the rodeo grounds. You may return to I-25 by staying on 354. If you choose this path, be sure to keep to the right when you have a choice. This route takes about 45 minutes. It joins I-25 at Bernardo (US-60, east), well north of Socorro. You may also simply return to Magdalena.

Originally Hispanic farmers from Polvadera, on the west bank of the Rio Grande, settled Riley[93]. The small valley and springs at the base of Ladron Peak made the

Santa Rita Catholic Church

Stone Schoolhouse at Riley

Disappearing New Mexico

area attractive for agriculture. The town was originally named Santa Rita, but the name had to be changed when it applied for a post office in 1892. The name Santa Rita had already been assigned to the copper mining community east of Silver City.

Mine closings, followed by overgrazing, and drought, spelled the end of Riley. The Santa Rita Church and the old stone schoolhouse remain. There is a picnic shelter near the church and several adobe ruins are nearby. One or two modern houses are in the area. Mass is held at the Santa Rita church once a year, on Memorial Day weekend during the Santa Rita Fiesta. The fiesta is a reunion for former residents and their descendants.

As you face the church, the cemetery is on the right. On the left is the lone grave of Daniel Bustamante[15]. The wooden cross bears the usual birth and death dates. Below the cross someone has attached a white piece of plywood containing more information about Bustamante's death: "Killed by bandits...." the text provides the names the bandits and suggests he was killed during a mail train robbery in Belen.

The actual truth is more interesting, as this may have been one of the last train robberies in the New Mexico. The robbery also tells quite a bit about lawlessness in the the old west.

During the early morning hours of May 23, 1898, Bronco Bill Waters and William "Kid" Johnson[96-101] went undetected when they boarded the southbound train pulling out of Belen. They quickly entered the engine cab and confronted the engineer and fireman with their pistols. About a mile and a half out of town they ordered the engineer to stop the train and one of the robbers jumped out and uncoupled the rear cars. With no one threatening them, the conductor and the express guard ran back to Belen to report the holdup

The robbers then ordered the engineer to proceed down the tracks for another mile and a half and then stop. The two then strapped several sticks of dynamite to the Wells Fargo safe and blew the side off it. After collecting scattered bills and

coins, the robbers threw a bag of coins into the cab of the engineer and fireman to share and disappeared into the night. The train crew proceeded to back up, reconnect the rear cars and return to Belen.

As it turned out, the robbers had stopped the train in Los Pueblitos, a short distance from a house where their horses were tied up. They packed up the loot, saddled up and road off toward the southwest. Although Wells Fargo downplayed the amount stolen, it is believed to have been in the $25,000 - 50,000 range.

Waters and Johnson traveled southwest to the Rio Salado and then turned northwest toward the Alamo Reservation. They had lunch and proceeded to a canyon at the base of Table Mountain, where they settled in for the night.

Deputies Francis X. Virgil and Daniel Bustamante came after them. Unfortunately, neither lawman brought a rifle. But they did follow the path the bandits had taken. Arriving at the Alamo Reservation, and since it was getting dark, they hired Navajo guides to help them stay on the trail. It was dark when they got to the bandit's camp, and they they decided to wait until light.

They tried to get within pistol range when the day broke, but were spotted. Pistols were no match for a rifle. Virgil and Bustamante and one of the guides were killed. The bandits fled. Then, two of the Navajos rode into Magdalena to fetch the Marshall. Bustamante's body was taken to his home in Santa Rita (now Riley), where he was buried. Due to decomposition, Virgil's body never made it home. His remains are buried at Los Lunas.

After the shootout the at the bandit's camp, Wells Fargo hired two lawmen who finally located the bandits in Greenlee County, Arizona. In the shootout there, Johnson received a fatal wound. Waters was wounded but survived. He was brought back to Santa Fe, where he was convicted of the killings and sentenced to life in prison.

After World War I broke out, Waters was released because of a manpower shortage at the prison. He returned to his old job at the Diamond A ranch near Hatchita. While repairing a windmill, a gust of wind came up and knocked him off. He died the next day and was buried there.

There are still a few occupied farms/ranches around Riley.

Disappearing New Mexico

Fort Craig (Socorro County)

Take I-25 to the San Marcial exit (174), then east over the Interstate, and south on old Highway 1 (about 11 miles). Then follow the signs to Fort Craig. If traveling on I-25 from the south, take Exit 115 and follow the signs.

One could also Exit I-25 at US-380, proceed to San Antonio, and turn south on NM-1. This takes you through the Bosque del Apache National Wildlife Refuge.

Fort Craig[102,103] isn't a ghost town. It was a major western military installation in the late 1800s. Its primary function was to control Apache and Navajo raids, and to protect the central portion of the Camino Real. The Fort saw action during the American Civil War[8,11,20,29,33], when the Confederacy attempted to separate the West from the Union, thereby gaining the gold and silver mines in California and Colorado, as well as supplies from seaports in southern California.

American Civil War

The southern half the New Mexico Territory, which included the southern portion of Arizona, was generally sympathetic to the Confederate cause. After seceding from the Union, a Regiment of Texas Mounted Volunteers captured Fort Bliss north of El Paso and prepared for a possible assault on Fort Fillmore, a Union installation near Mesilla, New Mexico. On July 24, 1861, Texans under the command of Lt. Col. John Baylor took Fort Fillmore without firing a shot. Baylor then rounded up about 400 Union soldiers fleeing Fort Fillmore, and he either pardoned them or con-

Command Quarters, Fort Craig

vinced them to join the Confederacy. Baylor also established a provincial government for the area, declared himself governor, and he appointed men to carry out the business of a new state. By all accounts his organization ran smoothly until 1862, when the army retreated to Texas.

Henry Hopkins Sibley, a West Point graduate and one time commander of Fort Union, convinced Jefferson Davis that it was important to capture the West. He was subsequently commissioned Brigadier General in the Confederate States Army. His orders were to "raise three full regiments of cavalry and to proceed with all possible dispatch to meet these conditions…." He was to lead 2,500 troops up the Rio Grande to capture Ft. Craig, Albuquerque, Santa Fe and Fort Union. With the fall of Fort Union, supply lines for the Confederacy, along with gold to purchase goods from Europe, would be assured.

Fort Craig's Commissary Walls - Black Mesa in Background

The Confederate army captured neither fort. In the south, Col. R.S. Canby shored up his defensive "might" by placing "Quaker" cannons (logs), rifles and empty soldier's caps beside real cannons and real soldiers along massive gravel bastions at Ft. Craig. Sibley believed his resources were inadequate to directly attack the fort and circled around Ft. Craig, attempting to cut off Union supplies from the north. In response, Canby started north to ensure that the fort would not become isolated.

On February 21, 1862, the two forces clashed at Val Verde (now Valverde) Crossing. Both sides sustained heavy losses, with the Confederates holding the battlefield and the Union retaining control of Ft. Craig. Col. Kit Carson, and his 1st New Mexico Volunteers, also fought on the Union side at Val Verde.

After Val Verde, the Confederate Army of New Mexico continued north and captured Albuquerque, where they set up headquarters in an abandoned warehouse.

Disappearing New Mexico

From Albuquerque they marched north, and took Santa Fe on March 10. From there the Confederates moved east along the Santa Fe Trail, intending to capture Fort Union.

On March 26, 1862 Confederate and Union forces first clashed at Glorieta Pass in an indecisive skirmish. Two days later, with reinforcements for both sides, the armies fought again, with the Union forced to withdraw. However, the battle of the "Gettysburg of the West" was hardly a Confederate victory. Union forces, led by Major Chivington, discovered the Confederate supply train. His troops burned eighty supply wagons and killed or scattered five hundred horses and mules. Without supplies the Confederate army was forced to return to Santa Fe and finally retreat south and back to Texas.

During their march toward Fort Union, the Confederates made several disastrous mistakes:

- Although desperately low on supplies, they chose to burn, rather than use, captured Union provisions.

- On two occasions, they lost supplies by not providing adequate protection for their wagons and animals. With these items their plan to capture Fort Union might have succeeded.

- They turned many Southern sympathizers against them by confiscating their property. As a result, during the journey back to Texas they received little local support and had to survive in a very hot and hostile land.

In 1993, a Congressionally appointed Civil War Sites Advisory Commission issued its "Report on the Nation's Civil War Battlefields." Glorieta Pass, along with Gettysburg, Antietam, and others, were named the ten most significant battlefields of the Civil War. It is now a unit of the National Park Service. The staff of the Pecos National Historical Park administers the portion of the battlefield that is on public land.

After the War

After the Civil War, Fort Craig returned to its original mission of controlling Indian attacks. It was headquarters for U.S. Army campaigns against Apaches. Troops from Fort Craig pursued the well-known Apache leaders Geronimo, Victorio, and Nana. The Fort was home to Buffalo Soldiers of the 9th Cavalry and 38th and 125th Infantry.

By the late 1870s, attempts to control Indian raiding were succeeding. The Western Apache were forced to abandon their homelands and move onto reservations. Conditions on the reservations, including disease, famine, cultural misunderstandings, and dishonest policies, triggered many escapes (see the Lincoln Wars in Chapter 3).

The most famous rebellion was the escape of the Warm Springs Apache, led by Victorio, and then by Nana. After seeing the decimation of their numbers on the reservations, Chief Victorio decided to escape from the San Carlos reservation and return his people to their homeland. Fort Craig became a staging area for the Army. On October 14, 1880, Victorio died at Tres Castillos, Mexico, where most of his band were either killed or captured by the Mexican Army. Eighty-year-old Nana then joined forces with Geronimo and continued to fight the Army for four more years.

When Geronimo and Nana surrendered in 1885, Fort Craig was permanently abandoned, its military function no longer needed. Nine years later, Fort Craig was sold at auction to the only bidder, the Valverde Land and Irrigation Company. In 1981, the property was eventually donated to the Bureau of Land Management by the Oppenheimer family. The site is now a BLM Special Management Area. It is listed on the National Register of Historic Places.

Fierro and Hanover (Grant County)

Both Hanover and Fierro can be reached by taking NM-152 through Hillsboro, driving past Kingston and continuing through the Gila National Forest. It's a pretty drive, but the mountain roads are steep and it's slow going. The drive to Hanover is about about 44 miles.

About two miles from Hanover, you will pass the huge Santa Rita copper mine on the left. Most people stop to look. Proceed until you cross the railroad tracks and turn right onto Hanover/Fierro Road.

About a mile up the road you encounter the ruins of the Hanover mines. Continue for another 3-4 miles to Fierro. Be careful when you cross the railroad tracks. Fierro is still an active mine site, and the railroad tracks are in use.

Alternatively, Hanover can be reached by taking US-180 north from Deming and turning right onto 152. Hanover/Fierro Road is about three miles to the east.

Hanover

Driving north on State Road 365 (Fiero Road), one finds the industrial remains of Hanover. Fierro and Hanover have a combined population of about 170. On the left is the mine's old office, and nearby is the mine's head-

Disappearing New Mexico

frame. About a mile up the road and to the right, is the Hanover Post Office. On the right, and about another half-mile, is a rusted old steel commercial building. To both sides of the road there are several private homes.

Abandoned Mine Office in Hanover

Headframe for a Hanover Mine

Storage Building at Hanover

Fierro

In another two miles we come to Fierro[104-106] and Saint Anthony's Catholic Church. Along the way, we pass a few dilapidated old houses. Most of the currently occupied residences are to the east of the road. The Phoenix Mercantile, an abandoned store of considerable size, is at 279 Fierro Road.

The Phoenix Mercantile

Abandoned Building - Fierro

Abandoned House - Fierro

Disappearing New Mexico

Another Abandoned Fierro Building

Behind Saint Anthony's Church, and sticking up above the cross, is the plant for processing ore. Stay alert in this area because there may be unexpected rail traffic.

The Chino or Santa Rita copper mine is about one mile east on NM-152. You might find it interesting. The mine is about 1.75 miles wide and 1,350 feet deep.

Pinos Altos (Grant County)

Pinos Altos is eight miles north of Silver City on NM-15. Take the Bear Creek Road from NM-15 and turn right onto Main Street at the second intersection. The Buckhorn, the Opera House and the Museum are ahead.

Pinos Altos[107-109] is an old mining town a few miles north of Silver City. In 1860, gold was discovered at Bear Creek, near what is now Pinos Altos. The town grew rapidly, but not without serious Apache attacks. As a result, miners left and did not return until troops were available after the Civil War.

In 1887 George Hearst came from California and purchased most of the Pinos Altos Mining District. He was also involved in building the Gold Avenue Methodist Church (now an art gallery). Other popular attractions include the Buckhorn Saloon, the Opera House, and the Pinos Altos Museum.

Since 1860 the Buckhorn Saloon has been a popular watering hole. It also has a small number of tables and functions as a restaurant. Reservations are advised (575-538-9911).

Buckhorn Saloon

Disappearing New Mexico

Pinos Altos Historic Museum

Like many of the old mining towns, the population of Pinos Altos is small. Today it only has about 375 people.

Old Pinos Altos Methodist Church
- Now an Art Museum

Pinos Alto Opera House

Hachita (Grant County)

Take I-10 to Exit 49 about (31 miles west of Deming) and turn south onto NM-146. Hachita is about 20 miles from I-10 at the intersection with NM-9.

Hachita[110] originally joined two railroads carrying copper ore from Arizona to refineries in El Paso. In response, a town with services grew up. However, as the demand for copper declined, so did shipments. The line from Morenci, Arizona stopped operating in 1934. The one from Douglas, Arizona pulled up its tracks in 1963. The town which once boasted a population of over 700, now has only 49. Hachita has a lot of interesting, abandoned buildings to see and photograph. Many of these are seriously dilapidated.

St. Catherine Mission Church

Another Abandoned House in Hachita

Several Abandoned Buildings in Hachita

Disappearing New Mexico

"My Church" in Hachita – At Least that's What the Sign Says

Cuchillo (Sierra County)

Take Exit 82 from I-25 (T or C Airport) and turn north on CR-181. In about 1.5 miles, turn left onto Highway 52. Continue on 52 for about 3-4 miles and you are in Cuchillo.

Cuchillo[111,112] is a small community of about 35 persons on NM-52. It's about seven miles west of the Truth or Consequences airport. Cuchillo isn't a destination. It's more like a stop on the road from Truth or Consequences to Winston or Chloride. A few people still live there, many of whom find work in nearby Truth or Consequences.

The Cuchillo Bar and Store, established in 1850, is said to be haunted. Strange noises are heard at night. It is also said that very few people are willing to enter the building after dark. For those who are both interested and fearless, the building is for sale.

Other interesting properties include the Saint Joseph Catholic Church and several dilapidated houses. We were particularly amused by the small replica of the Statue of Liberty found in one of the yards. As you can see, we named the image "Liberty Lost".

The For Sale Sign Has Been Up for Many Years
The Building Is Said to be Haunted

Liberty Lost

Saint Joseph Church

Disappearing New Mexico

Abandoned Dwelling in Cuchillo

Another Abandoned Dwelling

We Don't Know Its History, But the Building Had a Commercial Look.

In the ten years since we started this project, Cuchillo has changed considerably. Now (2023) the commercial building is gone, the church has a more neglected look, and our pet Statue of Liberty is missing. Also, we also didn't see signs of a restaurant. However, the "Old Cuchillo Bar and Store" is still for sale.

Winston (Sierra County)

Starting from Cuchillo, continue west on Highway 52 for about 22 miles, being sure to take the sharp left turn just past Red Hill. The Winston General Store is on the left. Turn onto Broadway in front of the store. Most of the interesting parts of town can be found along Broadway. The population of Winston is about 72.

Winston[113], which was once named Fairview, was born with the Black Hills silver mining boom. It was the business and social center of the area. It had a bank, a school, shops, and a stage that ran to the rail station in Engle. Engle is east and slightly south of the Elephant Butte Dam. Eagle is on CR-51.

A former miner named Frank Winston moved to Winston in 1882 and opened a successful mercantile. He was also a successful cattleman and the owner of the Fairview Garage. When silver mining ceased being profitable, Fairview fell on hard times. Most of the people moved on, but Frank Winston extended credit to his remaining neighbors, knowing he would probably never get paid back. After he died the locals changed the town's name to Winston in honor of his generosity.

Things to see in Winston include the schoolhouse. It's in a field to the east, several hundred yards down the dirt road called Main Street.

Winston's Schoolhouse

Disappearing New Mexico

The Fairview Garage is on the left, off Broadway. The garage has a rather unusual, pressed metal roof. Many pictures of Frank Winston's garage show an old tractor on the corner. The machine is gone now, but you can find it down the road in Chloride.

Old Fairview Garage

Building With Garden on Roof

An interesting old building is along Broadway. It has (or had) a substantial amount of vegetation growing on the roof.

Today, Winston is home to about 61 people.

Chloride (Sierra County)

To reach Chloride take Highway 52 through Chucillo and Winston. In front of the store in Winston turn south on Broadway until it bends to the right and intersects Republic Road (C006). Turn left and continue two miles. Then turn right onto Wall Street. It's about another mile to the center of Chloride.

Chloride[114-115] is a very interesting ghost town, where about 20 people continue to live. It started when Harry Pye found silver in 1879. Back then Chloride was a dangerous place. Apaches ambushed and killed many people, including Pye. Before the silver boom was over, Chloride had a bank, stores, and numerous saloons. Today, Chloride looks much as it did then. This is because Don and Dona Edmond purchased many of the buildings and have fixed them up. The museum is worth visiting, and the Doodle Dum house, with its history and unique construction, is especially interesting.

Doodle Dum was built in 1920 by Austin Crawford, who decided a heavy-duty structure would protect him should God display his wrath in the form of a hailstone storm. Crawford built the home by himself, carrying the stones from the

Doodle Dum House

Disappearing New Mexico

creek and personally putting each stone into place. He was about 80 years old at the time. Even more interesting is the fact that the four rooms are not connected internally. One must go outside to move from one to another. By 1923 Crawford had moved to the state psychiatric hospital in Las Vegas, NM. He remained there until his death.

Wall Street is the main drag through Chloride. Toward the end of Wall Street are the Pioneer Store Museum and the Monte Cristo Gift Shop & Gallery. The old tractor that used to stand beside the garage in Winston now sits to the right of the museum. The Chloride Bank-Café is on Wall Street. Across the street is the saloon.

Monte Cristo Saloon & Dance Hall, Gift Shop & Gallery

Old Tractor that Used To Be in Winston

The Star Saloon

The Chloride Bank & Cafe

Wall Street, at its west end, becomes the trail to the Chloride Canyon Petroglyphs. This is a rough trail. A four-wheel drive vehicle is highly recommended.

Disappearing New Mexico

Hillsboro (Sierra County)

From I-25, take Exit 63, turn on to NM-152 and drive about 17 miles to Hillsboro. Sadie Or-chard's Hotel (now the Black Range Museum) is on the left as you enter town. The remains of the old courthouse are on Elenora Street, one block up hill on the left.

Hillsboro[116] is home to about 154 people. Once the seat of Sierra County, Hillsboro was a mining town that started with the discovery of gold. It was also the stage for one of the more famous murder trials in New Mexico history. It was also the home of one of the most interesting women in western history. And, it hosted a second murder trial that caused controversy throughout the state.

The first trial involved the death of Albert Fountain and his son Henry. Fountain was a prominent Mesilla lawyer who had many powerful enemies.

Sadie Orchard ran a brothel, operated the Ocean Grove Hotel, and started a stage line. She was an occasional driver for the stage.

Due to the nature of the crime, the sentences imposed and the eventual outcome, the joint trial of Valentina Barilla and Alma Lyons divided people all over the New Mexico Territory.

The Fountain Trial

Fountain, was a Republican who championed statehood, something that un-doubtedly was delayed by New Mexico's lawlessness. With money and power, the Santa Fe Ring wanted to control New Mexico politics and was against statehood.

In 1896 Fountain, accompanied by 8-year-old son Henry, went to Lincoln to se-cure Grand Jury warrants for cattle rustling against 32. Fountain and his son never returned. The evidence suggested murder, but no bodies were never found.

Pat Garret, credited with killing Billy the Kid, finally arrested three men who were charged. On May 26, 1899, three years after the Fountains' disappearance, the trial of Oliver Lee and Jim Gililland took place in Hillsboro. Charges against William McNew had been dismissed previously on a technicality, but only after he spent a year in jail.

Thomas Catron was the prosecutor and Albert Fall was the defending attorney. After eighteen days and 75 witnesses the trial ended in acquittal. Jury deliberation took eight minutes.

In follow up: Lee was later elected to the New Mexico Senate. In 1912, Catron and Fall were elected as New Mexico's first US senators. In 1918, Catron was re-elected; Albert Fall wasn't. However, in 1921 Fall was appointed Secretary of the Interior by Warren G. Harding. He was later found guilty of accepting bribes in the Teapot Dome scandal. He was fined and spent the year of 1929 in prison.

Sadie Orchard's Hotel Where Most of the Dignitaries Stayed - It's Now a Museum

Sadie Creech Orchard (1859? - April 9, 1943)

Sadie Orchard may have been the most colorful woman in New Mexico's history[3]. She opened brothels, worked as a prostitute, started a stageline, and built and operated hotels and restaurants. Lawyers and other notables stayed in her hotel during the Fountain trial.

Sadie was born around 1860. She told people she was born in London, but it is more likely she was born in Iowa. When she arrived in Kingston in 1886, the town was enjoying the mining boom of the Black Range District. The potential for economic growth was enormous, and the district provided many opportunities to

Disappearing New Mexico

make a living. At that time, Kingston had a population of 5,000. The silver boon was in full swing, and dance halls and saloons were booming.

In Kingston in 1886, Sadie married a man named Orchard, who was frequently unemployed and had a "down and out" attitude on life. She later ran him off. Sadie was small, weighting about 100 pounds. She was said to be shapely, had black hair, blue eyes, and a small waist. She believed in dressing in the fashion of the times. She was also civic minded, raising money for a church in Kingston.

In the late 1880s, when Kingston's fortunes were fading, but Hillsboro's were prospering, Sadie moved her business. In Hillsboro she operated a bordello (at least one). She also built the Hillsboro Hotel (now the Black Range Museum). The hotel was said to set the best table in town. Several persons involved with the Fountain trial stayed there.

Sadie also started a stage line to Lake Valley, for which she occasionaly drove. At that time stagecoaches in the area were frequently harassed by Apaches, but she had no problems. Perhaps painting a picture of Victorio on each of the doors helped.

Sadie's humanitarian accomplishments were significant. In World War I, she tended to many less fortunate people. During the Spanish Flu epidemic of 1918, she nursed children, cared for the sick and dying, and helped lay out and bury the dead.

Sadie remained in Hillsboro for the rest of her life. She died there in 1943.

The Murder of Manuel Madrid[117]

Manuel Madrid moved to Hillsboro from Mexico. Later, he married a young Valentina Barilla, who was only fifteen years of age. Alma Lyons, a childhood friend, also came along with the deal. Valentina, being a bit of a flirt and good looking, caught the attention of Francisco Baca, a worker on Madrid's farm. The pair became infatuated with each other, and the die was cast.

The pair gave Alma some money, and she bought an arsenic product called "Rough on Rats". Valentina added the poison to Manual's coffee. It took several days for the poison to do its deed, but Manuel finally died on March 30, 1907. Dr. Frank Given, who was called to examine the body, decided death was due to arsenic poisoning.

The doctor's report was taken to a coroner's jury and both girls were charged with murder. When they testified before a justice of the peace, they also mentioned Baca's involvement. And the three became inmates at the Sierra County jail, all being indicted for first degree murder.

The girls were tried separately from Baca. Their trial concluded on May 9, 1907, with the jury taking less than an hour to find the pair guilty of first-degree murder. The next day, Judge Parker, who was almost apologetic, sentenced the two girls to hang.

Calls to change the sentences to life in prison came from all over the state. The Sierra County sheriff reported watching the girls in their cell, "playing and giggling like children of eight or ten years". He didn't believe they were of normal intelligence.

The Acting Governor Raynolds was disturbed by the sentence and sought council from important New Mexicans. Three days before the scheduled execution, Raynolds sent word that the sentences were commuted to life in prison.

Baca, on the other hand, had been in prison in Santa Fe, his trial being postponed until May 1908. In that trial, the jury could not agree on a verdict, resulting in a mistrial. The retrial took pace in May 1910. This time the jury found Baca not guilty due to insufficient evidence.

Governor Larrazolo commuted both women's sentences on May 12, 1919. The next year, on March 3, the women walked out of the penitentiary in Santa Fe. There were some restrictions, but they were essentially free. Valentina took a job on her brother's ranch in Parkview. In 1930, Alma was found in Santa Fe under the name Gaines.

The Courthouse

In 1937 the county seat moved from Hillsboro to Hot Springs. The old courthouse was torn down, with some of the bricks being sold and used for new construction. In 1950 Hot Springs, responding to a challenge from television host Ralph Edwards, changed its name to Truth or Consequences.

Window Shopping on Main Street

Disappearing New Mexico

Ruins of the Old Sierra County Court House

Door From Court House to Jail   A Good Place for Breakfast

Kingston (Sierra County)

From I-25 take Exit 63 onto NM-152, drive west through Hillsboro, cross Percha Creek, and on to Kingston. Just outside of Kingston, NM-152 forks and turns uphill and to the left. Stay to the right. Turn around if you see a cemetery on your right.

Kingston[118], on the eastern slopes of the Black Range, was the location of a major silver discovery in 1882. The town swelled to over 5,000 people, with grocery stores, hotels, saloons, and bordellos. It currently is home to about fifty people.

During the nineteenth century Kingston was the richest silver producer in New Mexico, producing almost 6,000,000 ounces of silver from 1883 to 1893. By the turn of the century its mines were exhausted, and people moved on. Kingston also suffered from fire and flood. Only three original buildings escaped destruction by fire. It almost happened again in 2013.

The old assay office is one of the buildings in Kingston that was spared by fire. Today it is a private residence. Two other buildings of interest are the Percha Bank and the Black Range Hotel. Because it was opened for minor construction, we obtained access to the Percha Bank.

Assay Office - Now a Private Residence

Apartments in Kingston

Disappearing New Mexico

The Percher National Bank

At the Teller's Window

The other Kingston property of interest is the Black Range Lodge (see below), which was built in the 1880's. The lodge is on the Main Street, to the west side of town. It is open to visitors. Call 575-895-5652 for information.

Lake Valley (Sierra County)

From NM-152 in Hillsboro take NM-27 south. It is 17 miles to Lake Valley.

You can also get to Lake Valley from NM-26, the road between Deming and Hatch by taking NM-27 north. The driving distance is 32 miles from Hatch and 42 miles from Deming.

Currently, no one resides in Lake Valley.

Silver[119-121] was discovered here in 1878. Along with Hillsboro and Kingston, Lake Valley was an important silver mining town. Its Bridal Chamber Mine once yielded almost pure silver, over 1.3 million oz. of it, with a single piece weighing about 7,000 oz. In 1893, when silver was devalued, the town survived on gold mining. The total output of silver from the Lake Valley mines was about 5,800,00 ounces. During WW II Lake Valley produced manganese. After the war, even the demand for that dried up. Lake Valley had a post office until 1955.

Mine and Buildings at Lake Valley

Disappearing New Mexico

The Bureau of Land Management offers walking tours from 9-4 every day except Tuesday and Wednesday. The site may be accessed on the other two days, but no employees or docents are available. Except for BLM caretakers, Lake Valley is completely abandoned. It is one of the true ghost towns in New Mexico.

This view shows the interior of the old schoolhouse that was built in 1904. It was used until 1960. Inside the old schoolhouse, half of the building is a one-room school. The room had the obvious teacher's desk and flags. Surprisingly it had both a piano and an organ. One schoolroom item we had never seen was double desks.

Inside the One-room School House - Note the Double Desks

Around the town were many old and dilapidated buildings. There is a church and a Conoco station from later in the town's history. This view shows the old stage stop for Sadie Orchard's line from Hillsboro. The building also served as a rail station. In the background are remnants of the manganese mines.

Miner's Residence

Trail Past the Water Tanks

Dilapidated House in Lake Valley

Old Cononco Station

Miner's Church

Disappearing New Mexico

Steins (Hidalgo County)

From Lordsburg, take I-10 west to Exit 3. Turn north onto Summit Road and you are there. The cemetery is south of the interstate on Cedar Mountain Road.

Currently, no one lives at Steins.

Steins, the "Ultimate American Ghost Town", [122-124] was closed in 2011, after the shooting death of its owner, Larry Link. The murder remains unsolved. In 2013 his family members announced that the ghost town would no longer be open to the public. However, in 2016 there was an indication that site might be open by appointment and on a limited basis. The Lordsburg-Hidalgo Chamber of Commere is a good contact (575-542-9864).

The building is the Steins Mercantile. In the background, cars and trucks can be seen moving along I-10.

Blades for a Windmill's Turban

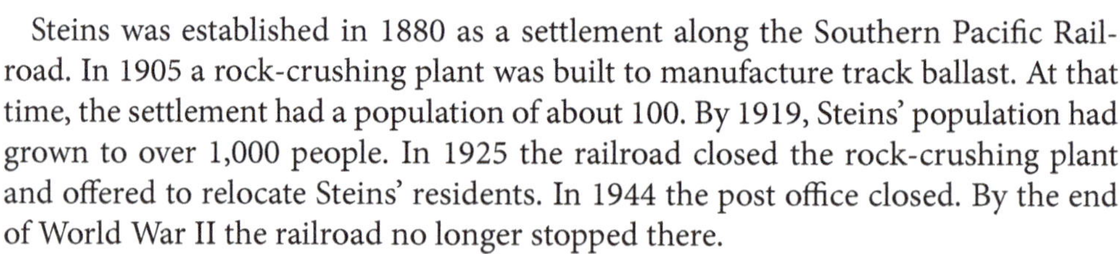

Steins was established in 1880 as a settlement along the Southern Pacific Railroad. In 1905 a rock-crushing plant was built to manufacture track ballast. At that time, the settlement had a population of about 100. By 1919, Steins' population had grown to over 1,000 people. In 1925 the railroad closed the rock-crushing plant and offered to relocate Steins' residents. In 1944 the post office closed. By the end of World War II the railroad no longer stopped there.

Shakespeare (Hidalgo County)

In Lordsburg, take Exit 22 from I-10 and turn South on to 494 (the extension of Main Street). Continue until you reach the fork just before the cemetery. Turn right onto Ghost Town Road (County Road A022) and again at the next fork. The gate to Shakespeare is ahead of you.

Shakespeare[125-127] was a silver mining town and a stop for the Butterfield Stage. At its peak, Shakespeare had 3,000 residents, a barbershop, hotels, saloons, and a laundry. When silver mining waned, the railroad by-passed Shakespeare. In 1932 the depression spelled the end. Shakespeare is on the National Register of Historic Places. The ghost town is about 7 miles south of Lordsburg. Currently, no one is living at Shakespeare.

For many years, Manny Hough lived and operated Shakespeare. It was open to the public on weekends in the summer. Manny's wife, Janaloo Hill, passed away in 2005. She is buried on the hill above Shakespeare. Manny continued to operate the site until 2016, when he also passed away.

The Grant House Stage Station

Shakespeare contains many old buildings. The images here include the Grant

Disappearing New Mexico

House Stage Station, several buildings with the remains of wagons in front, an inside view of the assay office, and a windmill, with its water tank. Our view of the assay office includes many tools of the trade.

Rusted Farm Wagon with the Stratford Hotel in the Background

Water Tank and Windmill

Lab Equipment in Assay Office

Southwestern Counties

Chance City (Luna County)

Chance City is about 3.5 miles south of the Bowlin's Butterfield Station 20 miles west of Deming on I-10.

Chance City[128] is a true ghost town. It is totally deserted. The old mining area is in a barren desert area south of I-10. Five or six crumbling stone structures remain. Silver was discovered here around 1880. The mining rights were later sold to George Hearst, owner of the San Francisco Examiner and father of William Hearst. Chance City grew to about 130 people.

One mineshaft, which runs about 200 feet into the hill, is still open, but it should be considered dangerous. Although the mines produced about $1.5 million in lead, silver, and gold, it and many others closed in 1886 when the price of lead declined.

The survival of this small mining town can be attributed more to the fact that the Southern Pacific Railroad's main line was only four miles away, rather than the small amounts of ore in the nearby mountains. Chance City is totally abandoned. Remains of rock and adobe buildings are scattered around the area. Some mine headframes are still standing. Most of the mine entrances have been sealed by the Bureau of Abandoned Mines (New Mexico). A natural gas pumping station is located nearby.

Ruins of a Stone Building

Disappearing New Mexico

Open Mine Shaft

Many mining towns died waiting for railroads, but several railroads altered their routes to accommodate the mines in the area. Chance City was lucky. When ore was discovered in the Victorio Mountains in the 1880's, the brand new Southern Pacific main line was only four miles away. That was the community's principal good fortune. However, only a modest half million dollars in gold, silver, copper, lead, and zinc were extracted from these, including the Last Chance. Mining efforts there lasted until the 1930's. The post office closed a year after it opened.

The image below shows the chute used to move ore to a wagon below. The image also shows how desolate the landscape is.

The emptiness of the southwestern New Mexico desert gives new meaning to the the toughness of the miners trying to eke out a living here.

Chute for Moving Ore
to a Wagon Below

Southwestern Counties

Columbus (Luna County)

Columbus is about 2.5 miles north of the Mexican border. It's a 33-mile drive from Deming on NN-11. Take Exit 82 from I-10. NM-11 is effectively the extension of US-180.

Columbus[129] was established in 1891, just across the border from Palomas, Chihuahua, Mexico. When the Southwestern railroad built a station about three miles to the north, the village moved. With an current estimated population of about 1,617, Columbus isn't really a ghost town. However, because of its history, it deserves mention.

Columbus Railroad Station - Now a Museum and Gift Shop

In 1916 Pancho Villa was upset because a Columbus shopkeeper refused to sell him guns. In retaliation, Villa staged a raid on the town. Villa's army burned part

Disappearing New Mexico

of the town and killed 10 civilians and 7 or 8 soldiers. As a result, Woodrow Wilson sent General John Pershing and 10,000 troops to pursue Villa. This was the first U.S. military use of motorized vehicles. They never caught Villa.

Camp Furlong Recreation Hall

Columbus has a few motels (the Los Milagros is reasonable) and restaurants. However, many visitors travel across the border and take their meals in Palomas. There are several good restaurants there. Because prices are lower in Mexico, many people also cross the border to purchase prescription drugs.

Conversely, many Mexican women choose to give birth in the U.S. and to have their children attend school in Deming, New Mexico. The children born there automatically become U.S. citizens. As is typical of most towns along the US-Mexican border, both sides of the border depend on one another.

Acknowledgements

MR would particularly like to thank Beth Meyer, his traveling companion to many of the southern counties. Without her company, these trips might not have occurred.

The following friends accompanied us on trips to photograph the various towns and communities featured in the book: Rebecca Bradshaw, Candy Carlson, Barbara Deaux, David Halpern, Arthur Lazar, Joey HolmesMeyer, Terry Maznio, David Sullinburger, Jerry Swetland, and Dianne Williams. Their company, patience, and encouragement are greatly appreciated.

We are particularly pleased to include Nancy Melin's images from Dead Horse Arroyo. These show the location where evidence of Folsom man was discovered. Likewise, Ben de Baca's photograph of the church at Loma Parda and his knowledge of the town's history are greatly appreciated. Except as noted, all photographs were taken by the authors.

Bill Tefft, with the Public Lands Information Center in Santa Fe, has been extrememly helpful. His knowledge of ghost towns and the many scenic places in the state is immense. Anyone interested in exploring New Mexico would do well to visit with Bill.

Special thanks are due to Elizabeth Martin, John Collison, Kathy Collison, Marilyn Fisher, Tricia West, Devan Ranganathan, and Susan Read for reviewing the text, catching many typographical errors, and making suggestions to improve the book. Without their efforts, this book would not have been possible. The authors are solely responsible for any remaining errors.

Disappearing New Mexico

1. Bardal, Jane, *Southwestern New Mexico Mining Towns*, Charleston, South Carolina: Arcadia Publishing, 2011, ISBN-13: 978-0-7385-7927-6.

2. Benson, Sara, *Lonely Planet Road Trip. Route 66*, Oakland, California: Lonely Planet Publications, 2003, ISBN-10: 1740595807.

3. Birchell, Donna Blake, *Wicked Women of New Mexico*, Charleston, SC, 2014, ISBN 978-1-62584-583-2.

4. Bial, Raymond, *Ghost Towns of the American West*, Boston: Houghton Mifflin, 2001, ISBN-10: 0618065571.

5. Boyle, Dixie, *Highway 60 & the Belen Cutoff: A Brief History*, Denver: Outskirts Press, 2010, ISBN-10: 1432760904, ISBN-13: 978-1432760908.

6. Burt, Olive Woolley, *Ghost Towns of the West*, New York: J. Messner, 1976, ISBN-10: 0671328034.

7. Carter, William, *Ghost Towns of the West*, Menlo Park, California: Lane Publishing Company, 1978, ISBN-10: 0376053127.

8. Colton, Ray C., *The Civil War in the Western Territories*, University of Oklahoma Press, 1959, ISBN 978-0-8061-1.

9. DeJauregui, Ruth E., *Ghost Towns*, New York: Crescent Books, 1988, ISBN-10: 0517658445.

10. Dulle, Ronald, *Tracing the Santa Fe Trail*, Missoula, Montana: Mountain Press Publishing Company, 2011, ISBN-13: 978-0-87842-571-6.

11. Edrington, Thomas S. and Taylor, John, *The Battle of Glorieta Pass*, Albuquerque: University of Ne w Mexico Press,1998.

12. Florin, Lambert, *New Mexico and Texas Ghost Towns*, Seattle: Superior Publishing Company, 1971.

13. Florin, Lambert, *Ghost Towns of the West*, New York: Promontory Press, 1993, ISBN-10: 0-88394-013-2.

14. Gardner, Mark L., *Fort Union National Monument*, Tucson, Arizona: Western National Parks Association, 2005, ISBN-10: 1-58369-054-9.

15. Defense Chiftan, Nov. 1, 2003.

16. Harris, Linda G., and Porter, Pamela, *Ghost Towns Alive*, Albuquerque: University of New Mexico Press, 2003, ISBN-10: 0-82-63-2908-X.

17. Hillerman, Tony, *The Great Taos Bank Robbery*, HarperCollins Publishers, Inc., New York, 1973.

18. Hinckley, James, *Ghost Towns of Route 66*, Minneapolis, MN: Voyager Press, 2011, ISBN-10: 0760338434, ISBN-13: 9780760338438.

19. Jenkinson, Michael, *Ghost towns of New Mexico: Playthings of the Wind*, Albuquerque: University of New Mexico Press, 1967.

20. King, Scottie, *Listen to the Wind: Ghost Towns of New Mexico*, Santa Fe, New Mexico: New Mexico Magazine, 1978.

21. Lawliss, Chuck, *Ghost towns, Gamblers & Gold*, New York: W.H. Smith Publishing. Co., 1985, ISBN-10: 0831739037, ISBN-13: 9780831739034.

22. Looney, Ralph, *Haunted Highways: The Ghost Towns of New Mexico*, Albuquerque: University of New Mexico Press, 1989, ISBN-10: 0826305067, ISBN-13: 9780826305060.

23. McKee, James C., *Narrative of the Surrender of a Command of U.S. Forces at Ft. Fillmore N.M. in July 186*1, Houston: Stagecoach Press, 1960.

24. Meleski, Patricia F., *Echoes of the Past: New Mexico's Ghost Towns*, Albuquerque: University of New Mexico Press, 082630219X.

25. Murphy, Lawrence R., *Lucien Bonaparrte Maxwell, Napoleon of the Southwest*, Norman Oklahoma: University of Oklahoma Press, 1983, ISBN-10: 9789040924.

26. Nolan, Fredrick, *The Lincoln County War*, Norman Oklahoma: University of Oklahoma Press, 1991, ISBN-10: 0-8061-2377-X.

27. Rakocy, Bill, *Mogollon Diary no. 2: and the Memory of Spiritual Chief: Geronimo*, El Paso, Texas: Bravo Press, 1988.

28. Pearce, T.M.,ed. *New Mexico Place Names: A Geographical Dictonary*, Albuquerque, University of New Mexico Press, 1965.

29. Sherman, James E., *Ghost Towns and Mining Camps of New Mexico*, Norman Oklahoma: University of Oklahoma Press, 1975, ISBN-10: 0806111062, ISBN-13: 9780806111063.

30. Ohio: Swallow Press, 1965, ISBN-10: 08-8040-0863-9.

31. Sperry, T.I., *Fort Union, A Photo History*, Tucson, Arizona: Western Parks and Monuments Association, 1991, ISBN-10: 1-877856-01-0.

32. Taylor, John, *Bloody Valverde: A Civil War Battle on the Rio Grande*, February 21, 1862, University of New Mexico Press, 1995, ISBN0-8263-2148-8.

33. Utley, Robert M., *Four Fighters of Lincoln County*, Albuquerque: University of New Mexico Press, 1986, ISBN-10: 0-8263-0897-X.

34. Varney, Philip, *New Mexico's Best Ghost Towns*, Albuquerque: University of New Mexico press, 1987, ISBN-10: 0-8263-1010-9, ISBN-13: 978-0-8263-1010-1.

35. Webb, Todd, *Gold Strikes and Ghost Towns*, Garden City, N. Y.: Doubleday, 1961.

36. Wolle, Muriel Sibell, *The Bonanza Trail: Ghost Towns and Mining Camps of the West*, Bloomington: Indiana University Press, 1953.

37. Wolle, Muriel Sibell, *The Bonanza Trail: Ghost Towns and Mining Camps of the West*, Bloomington: Indiana University Press, 1953.

38. Woods, Dora Elizabeth Ahern, *Ghost Towns and How to to Get to Them*, Santa Fe, New Mexico: The Sunstone Press, 1978, ISBN-10: 0-913270-30-X.

Disappearing New Mexico

39.   Zolbrod. Paul G., ***Diné Bahanè, TheNavajo Creation Story***, Albuquerque, New Mexico, University of New Mexico Press, 1984, ISBN 0-8263-1043-5.

The following are references to web pages. These require ongoing financial support from the posting organization. Without that they may disappear.

References to places described in the Wikipedia are not included.

40.   https://geoinfo.nmt.edu/tour/landmarks/cabezon/home.html

41.   https://cityofdust.blogspot.com/2018/01/music-on-wind-guadalupe-new-mexico.html

42.   https://fourcornersgeotourism.com/entries/guadalupe-ruin-chacoan-outlier/
5c2a8872-ec3a-4176-a718-294708f29d1

43.   https://www.newmexico.org/places-to-visit/ghost-towns/cerrillos/

44.   https://wandernewmexico.com/blog/madrid-new-mexico-hidden-gem-on-the-turquoise-trail

45.   https://www.newmexico.org/places-to-visit/ghost-towns/hagan/

46.   https://www.newmexico.org/places-to-visit/ghost-towns/elizabethtown/

47.   https://www.legendsofamerica.com/nm-cimarron/

48.   https://www.legendsofamerica.com/rayado-new-mexico/

49.   https://www.legendsofamerica.com/nm-dawson/

50.   https://www.legendsofamerica.com/folsom-new-mexico/

51.   https://www.legendsofamerica.com/sugarite-canyon-new-mexico/

52   https://www.legendsofamerica.com/la-cueva-new-mexico/

53.   http://historic-trails.unm.edu/sites/la-cueva-historic-district.html

54.   https://www.newmexico.org/places-to-visit/ghost-towns/loma-parda/

55.   https://el-camino-real.smugmug.com/Ghost-Towns/New-Mexico-Ghost-Towns/Loma-Parda-NM/

56.   https://www.codypolston.com/loma-parda-nm-history/

57.   https://www.nps.gov/nr/travel/american_latino_heritage/watrous_la_junta.html

58.   https://www.legendsofamerica.com/tiptonville-new-mexico/

59.   https://www.nps.gov/foun/index.html

60.   https://www.legendsofamerica.com/nm-fortunion/

61.   http://npshistory.com/publications/foun/index.html

62.   http://historic-trails.unm.edu/sites/la-cueva-historic-district.html

63.   https://www.legendsofamerica.com/la-cueva-new-mexico/

64. http://www.coloniasnm.com/about.html

65. https://www.legendsofamerica.com/dilia-new-mexico/

66. https://www.wikiwand.com/en/Anton_Chico,_New_Mexico

67. https://www.onlyinyourstate.com/new-mexico/ghost-town-of-cuervo-nm/

68. https://cityofdust.blogspot.com/2013/06/where-crows-flew-cuervo-new-mexico.html

69. https://www.theroadwanderer.net/66NMex/newkirk.htm

70. https://www.legendsofamerica.com/nm-sanjon/

71. https://www.legendsofamerica.com/tx-glenrio/

72. https://www.texasstandard.org/stories/how-a-bad-survey-and-powerful-connections-added-1000-square-miles-to-texas-lands

73. https://cityofdust.blogspot.com/2013/06/cross-road-blues-vaughn-new-mexico.html

74. https://cityofdust.blogspot.com/2013/08/the-last-hanging-crime-duran-new-mexico.html

75. https://www.newmexico.org/places-to-visit/ghost-towns/ancho/

76. https://www.legendsofamerica.com/nm-ancho/

77. https://www.legendsofamerica.com/nm-jicarilla/

78. https://www.legendsofamerica.com/nm-whiteoaks/

79. https://newmexiconomad.com/white-oaks/

80. https://nmhistoricsites.org/fort-stanton

81. https://nmhistoricsites.org/lincoln

82. https://newmexiconomad.com/billy-the-kid (New Mexico Nomad, The Short Life & Legion of Billy the Kid)

83. https://www.legendsofamerica.com/nm-lincoln/

84. https://cityofdust.blogspot.com/2011/12/life-and-death-by-railroad-yeso-new.html

85. https://pinintheatlas.com/travel-blogs/yeso-new-mexico/

86. https://www.hiddennewmexico.com/blog/dripping-springs

87. https://www.blm.gov/sites/blm.gov/files/docs/2021-08/NM_DrippingSpringsHistory_2020%28508%29.pdf

88. https://www.newmexico.org/places-to-visit/ghost-towns/mogollon/

89. https://newmexiconomad.com/mogollon/

90. https://www.legendsofamerica.com/nm-mogollon/

91. https://westernmininghistory.com/towns/new-mexico/mogollon/

92. https://www.onlyinyourstate.com/new-mexico/old-mining-town-sinister-history-nm/

93. https://www.newmexico.org/places-to-visit/ghost-towns/magdalena/

94 https://www.newmexico.org/places-to-visit/ghost-towns/kelly/

95. https://westernmininghistory.com/towns/new-mexico/kelly/

96. https://www.ghosttowns.com/states/nm/riley.html

97. https://hyse.org/pdf/www.aoc.nrao.edu/~pharden/hobby/BBILL1.pdf

98. https://www.legendsofamerica.com/bronco-bill-walters/

99. https://tomrizzo.com/road-agent/

100. https://www.travelblog.org/North-America/United-States/New-Mexico/Belen/blog-1047808.html.

101. https://cityofdust.blogspot.com/2013/12/a-town-with-two-names-riley-new-mexico.html

102. https://www.nps.gov/articles/000/new-mexico-fort-craig.htm

103. https://www.roadunraveled.com/blog/fort-craig-civil-war-battlefield-new-mexico/

104. https://www.newmexico.org/places-to-visit/ghost-towns/hanover-fierro/

105. https://www.newmexico.org/places-to-visit/ghost-towns/hanover-fierro/

106. https://cityofdust.blogspot.com/2015/04/iron-town-fierro-new-mexico.html

107. https://www.newmexico.org/places-to-visit/ghost-towns/pinos-altos/

108. https://www.desertusa.com/desert-new-mexico/pinos-altos.html

109. https://newmexiconomad.com/pinos-altos/

110. https://www.historynet.com/ghost-town-old-hachita-new-mexico/

111. https://sierracountynewmexico.info/attractions/cuchillo-new-mexico/

112. https://newmexiconomad.com/cuchillo-new-mexico/

113. https://sierracountynewmexico.info/attractions/winston-new-mexico/

114. https://sierracountynewmexico.info/attractions/chloride-new-mexico/

115. https://newmexiconomad.com/chloride-new-mexico/

116. https://www.newmexico.org/places-to-visit/ghost-towns/hillsboro/

117. http://hillsborohistory.blogspot.com/2012/03/poisoning-at-hillsboro.html

118. https://www.newmexico.org/places-to-visit/regions/southwest/kingston/

119. https://sierracountynewmexico.info/attractions/lake-valley-new-mexico/

120. https://newmexiconomad.com/lake-valley-new-mexico/

121. https://westernmininghistory.com/towns/new-mexico/lake_valley_nm/

122. https://www.legendsofamerica.com/nm-steins/

123. https://www.ghosttowns.com/states/nm/steins.html

124. https://cityofdust.blogspot.com/2014/02/troubled-times-steins-new-mexico.html

125. https://www.newmexico.org/places-to-visit/ghost-towns/shakespeare/

126. https://www.shakespeareghostown.com/

127. https://www.legendsofamerica.com/nm-shakespeare/

128. http://www.westernghosttowns.com/chance.htm

129. https://www.newmexico.org/places-to-visit/regions/southwest/columbus/

Disappearing New Mexico

Notes

Dissapering New Mexico